P9-CDL-964

APPALACHIAN FALL

APPALACHIAN FALL

Dispatches from Coal Country on What's Ailing America

JEFF YOUNG

and the Ohio Valley ReSource

TILLER PRESS

New York London Toronto Sydney New Delhi

An Imprint of Simon & Schuster, Inc.
1230 Avenue of the Americas
New York, NY 10020

First Tiller Press hardcover edition August 2020

Interior design by Laura Levatino

Manufactured in the United States of America

3 5 7 9 10 8 6 4 2

Library of Congress Cataloging-in-Publication Data

Names: Young, Jeff (Journalist), author.
Title: Appalachian fall : dispatches from coal country on what's ailing America / by Jeff Young.
Description: New York : Tiller Press, [2020] | Includes bibliographical references and index.
Identifiers: LCCN 2020000867 (print) | LCCN 2020000868 (ebook) | ISBN 9781982148867 (hardcover) | ISBN 9781982148874 (ebook)
Subjects: LCSH: Appalachian Region—Social conditions—21st century. | Appalachian Region—Economic conditions—21st century. | Appalachian Region—Politics and government—21st century.
Classification: LCC HN79.A127 Y68 2020 (print) | LCC HN79.A127 (ebook) | DDC 306.09756/8—dc23
LC record available at https://lccn.loc.gov/2020000867
LC ebook record available at https://lccn.loc.gov/2020000868

ISBN 978-1-9821-4886-7
ISBN 978-1-9821-4887-4 (ebook)

To all who make public media possible.

Contents

Preface

WE DIDN'T YET have cable when I was growing up on Malcolm Lane in Wayne County, West Virginia, but I still managed to watch far more television than any kid probably should. The rooftop antenna pulled down three fuzzy channels, maybe four on a good day, but they delivered local commercials and jingles so effectively that I can clearly recall many today. There was a dancing cartoon pig with a top hat and cane who sold meat. There was a car dealership with giant American flags (the kind of dealership where my father would later work).

There was also one commercial that I often thought of as I worked on this book. It was an ad for the state's coal industry. Even as a kid, I remember thinking it odd that the coal companies would run TV commercials. Did they think I could pop to the store and buy a lump of coal? What were they selling, exactly?

The ad made mining look heroic (as it is, in many ways). As a group of miners emerged from a dark portal, music swelled and a male chorus delivered the ad's anthemic message:

"Coal! Is West Virginia!"

Not just "part of," mind you. Not just "important to." "*Is*."

As in: one *does not exist* without the other.

It was a bold statement. But I doubt many people watching at the time would have argued. If any industry could lay claim to actually *being* an entire state, surely it was this one. Coal ran deep in the state's economy, politics, and history. The same is true for many other parts of Appalachia, which have been at the mercy of resource extraction for more than a century.

As I learned about and reported on the coal industry's many ill effects over the years, from gob piles to global warming, the old song took on a different, darker tone for me. It carried a not-so-subtle message for anyone who would question the industry or propose an alternate vision of what West Virginia or Appalachia might be.

Only then did I begin to realize what that commercial was really selling: a belief system. The belief that no matter how much damage mining did to the land, water, air, and people, it was a small cost compared to the thought of life without coal.

If coal *is* your place, then without it, what are you?

THAT IS ONE of the questions the Ohio Valley ReSource has been trying to answer for the past four years. The ReSource is a regional journalism collaborative established in 2016, when seven public media outlets in Kentucky, Ohio, and West Virginia formed a partnership. With funding from the Corporation for Public Broadcasting, these stations hired a team of eight journalists. These public media partners are helping to restore local journalism in underserved communities, where, in many cases, the contraction of the newspaper industry has left "news deserts."

The ReSource is also helping to tell the region's story to national audiences in a way that is rooted in and authentic to the communities we serve. Rural communities, and Appalachians in particular, are often wary of how they are portrayed in the national media, and with good reason.

Because the ReSource reporters live and work in the places they cover, the resulting narratives better reflect the complexities, history, and nuances of those communities. We do not flinch from the many problems here, but we remain open to the solutions, and we recognize our subjects as people with agency, not simply victims of circumstance. As a friend once told me, journalism should be something that happens *in* a place, not something that happens *to* a place.

This book draws upon that body of reporting to explore the health, work, and environment of a place undergoing extraordinary change. Coal, heavy manufacturing, and agriculture, the very vertebrae of Appalachian employment, are all in wrenching transformation, and with that, the region's traditional, rural ways of life are also changing. For many, those changes are not for the better.

Most of what you read here comes from stories directly reported by the ReSource team and our occasional partner on investigative work, NPR. Any information that draws upon other work is noted as such. We learned a lot in researching these pieces, and we hope you will do the same in reading them.

ONE IMPORTANT THING we have learned is that the very name "Appalachia" is so fraught with stereotype that it is often hard to see it with clear eyes, especially in this political moment. We hope to offer some clarity in these pages by spotlighting a diversity of regional perspectives and experiences. But we must ask a favor of you, dear reader. Please set aside any notions that you may have about Appalachia as a place apart, and consider it, instead, as a part of America.

In fact, we argue here that the resolution to many of America's most pressing challenges lies in better understanding and addressing Appalachia's conundrum.

If we are really serious about climate change, for example, the solutions must include those people who fear they have the most to lose in a clean-energy transition. If automation displaces more workers, as many experts predict, there are likely important lessons from a place experiencing mass economic displacement. And if we are to fully reckon with the rising effects of income inequality or the mounting toll from an addiction epidemic, does it not make sense to look to a place that has been dealing with those very things for decades?

Here's another thing that we have learned. That old coal industry slogan—that this place is nothing more than coal—isn't true. There was an Appalachia long before the coal industry and there will be one long after the last mine closes. The question is, what will that Appalachia be? And will other Americans recognize that their fates, too, are tied to its future?

—Jeff Young, on behalf of the ReSource team

APPALACHIAN FALL

1.
Welcome to Appalach-America

CHARLES WAYNE STANLEY ran underground mining machines for some twenty years, cutting coal from beneath the hills where Virginia meets Kentucky along the Cumberland Ridge. He spent another decade or so as a roof bolter, work that kept the rock above from falling in on his fellow miners.

By age fifty-three, when the ReSource and NPR interviewed him, Stanley was disabled and no longer mining. But in his heart he was still and would always be a miner. Listen to Stanley and you'll hear a common coal country refrain.

"It's time that we be recognized for what we have contributed." America owes its coal miners, Stanley said, for the sacrifices they made to provide the country power.

"It was coal miners that put this nation on the map," Stanley said, growing agitated. "Without coal there would have been no Industrial Revolution, there would be no New York City, nothing on these grounds of this United States, this great nation we live in, if it hadn't come from the back of a coal miner."

Miners like Stanley are a proud lot, and rightly so. Billions of dollars in mineral wealth flowed out of Appalachia, on barges moving down the Ohio River to power stations, on trains winding north to steel mills. Coal fueled the Industrial Revolution and the great war machine that defeated facism.

But in the early twenty-first century, as America moves away from its nineteenth-century fuel, the place that powered the nation is falling further behind in key measures of health and wealth. Amid the collapse of a keystone industry and the rise of an addiction epidemic, many parts of coal country are at risk of falling apart.

Like much of rural America, Appalachia is still awaiting recovery from the Great Recession of 2008. Compared to the country's urban centers, employment and income lag further behind in rural areas, a division that economists say has been growing since the 1980s. But the problems are more acute in coal country.

The Appalachian Regional Commission, a federal-state partnership, issues an annual report on progress toward its goal of putting the region on par with the rest of the country. The report places county economies along a continuum of five stages, from "distressed" to "attainment." In the most recent fiscal year, 80 of the 420 counties in Appalachia are in "economic distress."[1] That means those counties have a mix of low per capita income and high rates of poverty and unemployment far beyond what most of the country experiences, placing them among the worst 10 percent of county economies in the nation.

Most of these distressed counties—more than sixty of them—are in the heart of the coal-producing region where Kentucky, Ohio, Virginia, and West Virginia meet. Another forty-seven counties in coal country are merely "at risk," ranking between the worst 10 and 25 percent of counties in the nation. A few luckier ones are "in transition," or getting closer to national averages. But in its latest measure the ARC found eighteen counties—mostly coal-producing ones—moving in the wrong direction, falling further back toward distress.

For the most part, the places that produced the most coal are those most mired in poverty, and they continue to fall further behind the rest of the country, even as the national economy expands.

For example, in its most recent report, the ARC found per capita market income increased and poverty rates improved slightly in Appalachia in recent months. But those improvements happened at a much slower pace than in the rest of the country, such that the income and poverty gaps between Appalachia and the nation as a whole grew even wider.

The region is also losing ground in many key health indicators; mortality rates are rising in some parts of the region and people can now expect to live shorter lives than their parents.[2] Some counties in coal country have an average life expectancy on par with nations such as Bangladesh.

Poor health and poverty are not new in Appalachia, of course. Coal country is well accustomed to the hardships of resource extraction and the boom-bust cycles that have defined its fortunes. But this time is different.

Despite political rhetoric about a "coal comeback," the statistics are clear that coal jobs are dwindling and, for most of Appalachia, they are not coming back.

And it's not just the jobs. The revenue that local governments depended upon to fund schools and basic services is also largely gone. Taxes on mining and the value of unmined minerals plummeted as more coal companies went bankrupt. Many county governments in coal country face the risk of complete fiscal collapse. Boone County, in southern West Virginia, is among the most coal-reliant counties in the nation. Mining activity there fell some 70 percent from 2012 to 2017, and property and severance tax revenues dropped by more than a third. Boone County closed some public schools and limited basic services such as waste disposal.[3]

The coal bankruptcies keep piling up. By some estimates, two-thirds of the coal mined in the country now comes from companies that are in or just recently emerging from bankruptcy.

Some coal companies in a slump simply refuse to pay overdue taxes to state and local governments. This was the case with the companies belonging to coal baron billionaire Jim Justice and his children, which for several years failed to pay millions in state and local taxes for coal mines in Kentucky, Virginia, West Virginia, and two other states. That forced some strapped communities to make deep cuts in crucial services.

In 2016, when NPR and the ReSource first reported on the Justice companies, they owed roughly $15 million in a combination of overdue taxes to several states and delinquent mine safety fines to the federal government.[4]

While the Justices are not the only mining-company owners seeking to avoid or delay taxes and fines, two things set their mines apart. The Justice companies owed far more in overdue mine safety fines than any other coal companies in the nation, and, at the time, Jim Justice was also the Democratic candidate for governor of West Virginia. He won, and, years later, the Justice companies finally started to pay back some of the millions in overdue tax payments. In 2019, the Department of Justice sued the Justice companies to try to recover more than $4 million in overdue mine safety fines.[5]

But by then, of course, the damage was done. County governments had gone years without the revenue, and many were forced to make painful cuts. A report from the Brookings Institution warns that many coal-dependent communities face a "fiscal death spiral" as the last mines close: revenue dries up, services are cut, and more people move away, further eroding home prices and the local tax base.

The coal money is gone. Gone down those tracks, gone along those rivers, gone into the pockets of coal executives who now turn their attention to other pursuits, such as politics and luxury properties.

Jim Justice financed his successful run for governor in West Virginia, and his family owns the luxury Greenbrier resort, which hosts events by the state's coal industry and congressional Republicans. Former Massey Energy CEO Don Blankenship, who served a year in prison for conspiracy to violate mine safety standards after the 2010 explosion that killed twenty-nine of his miners, has put his fortune into a run for the US Senate in West Virginia and is now mounting a third-party run for president.

Ohio coal executive Bob Murray, whose company filed for bankruptcy in 2019, helped set Trump administration policy with a wish list of rollbacks to worker safety and environmental protections. Kentucky coal executive Joe Craft and his wife, Kelly, gave more than $8 million in political contributions to federal candidates over the years, including approximately $2 million to Donald Trump's campaign and inauguration.[6] Kelly Craft is now Trump's envoy to the United Nations.

Even some smaller industry players have parlayed coal wealth into high-profile real estate. Coal company executive Jeff Hoops, for example, owned a coal company called Blackjewel whose bankruptcy in 2019 was so abrupt that it left more than a thousand Appalachian miners without their final paychecks. Blackjewel miners staged a desperate demonstration on railroad tracks in Kentucky's Harlan County, blocking a last load of Hoops's coal in order to demand their back pay. Hoops, meanwhile, was planning a luxury hotel and resort with a Roman theme, complete with a theater designed after the Colosseum. Hoops calls the resort the Grand Patrician.

Even when the coal money was flowing, the region's political leadership often lacked the will or ability to harness that revenue to support the sort of things communities sorely need now, such as better schools and basic infrastructure improvements.

Martin County, in eastern Kentucky, is perhaps the readiest example. The mining communities there dug enough coal over the past century to power eighty million homes and make millionaires of some local mine owners. But Census data shows that nearly 40 percent of Martin Countians live below the poverty line, and for years the county government has been unable to even reliably deliver a clean glass of water to many residents.

Until recently, the county's aging water system lost more water to leaks than it sent through faucets. Customers complained of frequent service interruptions and discolored water, and their bills came with a notice that drinking the water could increase the risk of cancer. By the time the water system reached a state of crisis in 2016, the coal money that might have paid for repairs and upgrades was largely gone.

Across Appalachia the final, full price of providing coal is coming due just as the industry winds down and seeks to unload its legacy costs onto the public. As more coal companies "shed" debts in bankruptcy, miners often lose health and retirement benefits. The federal fund that pays medical costs for miners sickened by black lung is falling into billions of dollars of debt. State environmental officials cast anxious eyes on the mounting bills for reclamation of old surface mines, costs that will likely fall on taxpayers.

Coalfield activists here use the term "energy sacrifice zone" to describe the places where they live and work. Mountaintops were flattened, streams poisoned, and men and women laid low in order to provide the black rock and its few flickering moments of heat and light. The direct cost of Appalachia's contribution to the country can be measured in damaged lands and diseased lungs.

Black lung, a preventable occupational disease caused by exposure to the coal and rock dust in mines, is roaring back in Appalachia, as a two-year investigation by NPR and the ReSource showed. NPR's survey of medical and legal clinics in six Appalachian states found more than 2,300 miners have the most advanced form of the disease.[7] Government health researchers later confirmed that black lung is at a twenty-five-year high, afflicting one in five experienced miners in the region.[8]

If a sick miner is fortunate enough, and fights long enough, he or she might overcome the obstacles of an industry-influenced bureaucracy to win black lung benefits. That might pay for a million-dollar lung transplant, which can gain a miner a few more years of breath. But there is no cure for this progressive and ultimately fatal disease.

Charles Wayne Stanley is a living, breathing example of this particular sacrifice. He made his point of pride about miners and their contributions to the country while visiting Stone Mountain Health Services clinic in Virginia, which serves miners with black lung. Stanley has been diagnosed with the worst form of the disease.

"Staying on oxygen twenty-four seven. Dying of suffocation. That's what I got to look forward to," he said. "I've seen it too many times in coal miners."

Stanley watched his uncle and his wife's grandfather take their last breaths, "eat up with black lung," he said.

"You see more and more people now with the rock dust and black lung. Lot younger too. Used to be an old miners' disease; now it's young people."

Listen to Stanley. Consider his condition, and that of his community. If you do, some tough questions soon follow: What does America owe to this place that helped the country rise? And what are the implications for the country if Appalachia is simply left behind in its fall?

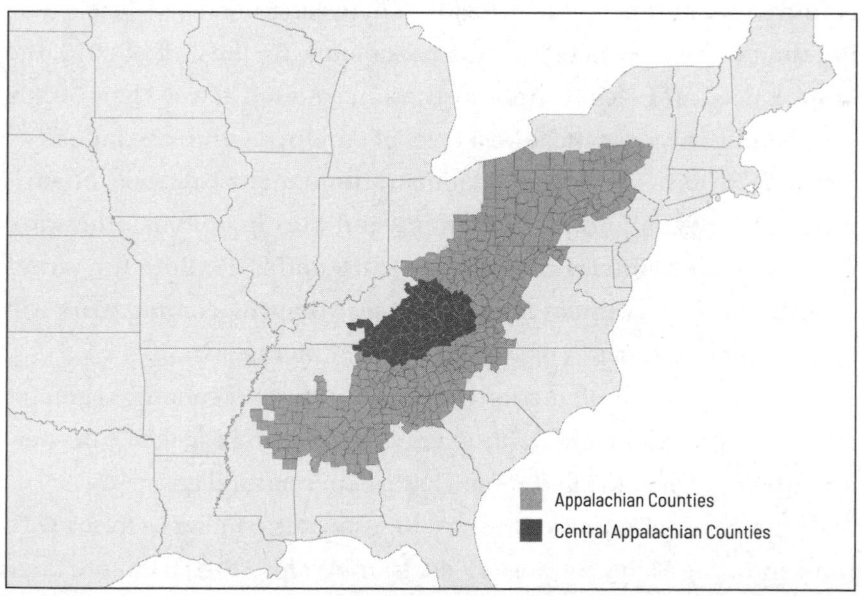

Appalachia spreads across parts of thirteen states, from southern New York to central Alabama. The heart of the region—central Appalachia—includes eastern Kentucky, southeastern Ohio, the western counties of Virginia, and much of West Virginia.

TWO YEARS AFTER his election, President Donald J. Trump returned to one of his most fervent bases of support for another campaign-style rally. In Huntington, West Virginia, he took the stage of the Big Sandy Arena, named for a local discount furniture business, which, in turn, is named for a nearby river that flows through the heart of what was once called the "billion-dollar coalfield" of southern West Virginia.

"We've ended the war on beautiful, clean coal," Trump told the crowd. "And we're putting our coal miners back to work."

But as is often the case with Trump's claims, the facts tell a different story. West Virginia did enjoy a modest bump in mining employment because of a temporary increase in coal exports used for steelmaking, but coal is not coming back as an American fuel source.

Federal government figures show total coal employment in the country was, at best, holding steady at between 51,000 and 53,000 during the first two years of Trump's presidency. By the end of 2019, the Mine Safety and Health Administration counted fewer than 50,400 coal employees, near the lowest level of employment in the industry's history.[9] Despite the Trump administration's many rollbacks of environmental regulations on the mining and burning of coal, the wave of mining bankruptcies continued in 2018 and 2019. Both the power industry and government agencies project that the coming years will bring still more closures of coal-fired power plants.[10]

This is primarily a function of changing energy economics, greater efficiency, growth in renewable energy sources, and especially the new abundance of cheaper and somewhat cleaner natural gas.

Muhlenberg County, in western Kentucky, is coming to terms with the Tennessee Valley Authority's decision to close the last of the large coal burners at its Paradise fossil station. The place was made famous by John Prine's song "Paradise" as the home of a ruined landscape that "Mister Peabody's coal train" had hauled away.

Today at Paradise a gleaming new high-efficiency generator burns natural gas to turn turbines for power. Despite the protests of Kentucky's governor and tweets from President Trump urging the TVA to keep coal power in place, the utility stood by its decision. Burning coal is a losing proposition, and many utilities are eager to phase it out altogether.

The Tennessee Valley Authority's Paradise Fossil Plant in Muhlenberg County, Kentucky. The coal-burning units in the background, in operation since 1963, are being replaced by the new, billion-dollar gas-fueled unit in the foreground.

That leaves many towns wrestling with what their future will be once the coal burners power down. In eastern Ohio's Coshocton County, American Electric Power is closing its Conesville power station years earlier than the utility had initially scheduled. AEP is one of the country's largest coal-burning utilities, and even it cannot wait to reduce its coal business.

As with coal mine closures, the county governments and school systems that hosted power plants are bracing for major blows to their budgets as the revenue that had sustained the local economy for decades disappears. Coshocton officials host worker training and education events, coaching longtime coal plant workers through the finer points of résumé writing and job interviews, skills many have not needed since they walked through the power plant doors years earlier.

But in Coshocton and other communities looking to turn the corner after coal's collapse, all the worker training efforts do not generate jobs for those workers. Coal-dependent communities are struggling to fill the void of lost jobs and revenue and to build new, diverse economic opportunities. After a century of domination by a single extractive industry, many of these places are now saddled with the legacy costs of mining and burning coal and suffering from inadequate investment in infrastructure and education.

The effect is more than just a loss of jobs and revenue; it is a loss of health and hope, manifesting in shorter life spans, increased misery, and a growing politics of demagoguery and division that all have effects far beyond the region.

"If we don't pay attention to the economic hurt of extraction communities and invest in solutions that show there is a viable path forward, we'll only deepen the division in our country," Brandon Dennison said from a witness table in the US Capitol.

Dennison is founder and CEO of Coalfield Development Corporation, a nonprofit in southern West Virginia that retrains workers and helps new businesses get off the ground. He and others working to diversify local economies in the wake of coal's collapse had been asked to advise a House committee on how to make the transition to new energy work for those who labored in the old energy economy.

"We in Appalachia need to know we are valued, and the country needs to know we have more to offer than just coal," Dennison said.

	Appalachia	United States
Percent population change, 2000–2010	**6.8%**	**9.7%**
Average income in 2017, as a percentage of U.S. average	**20% less**	**–**
Average unemployment rate, 2015–2017	**5.4%**	**4.8%**
Average poverty rate, 2013–2017	**16.3%**	**14.6%**

AMERICA HAS LONG considered Appalachia a backwater. Geographic isolation and a unique mountain culture gave rise to stereotypes that made it easy to construct a sort of gated community of the mind in which Appalachia is kept apart from mainstream America. Often, the dominant cultural narratives present Appalachian people as somehow to blame for the pervasive poverty and social problems they endure.

Even supposedly sympathetic portrayals are often premised on the notion that some underlying cultural flaws explain the region's woes. In J. D. Vance's bestselling memoir, *Hillbilly Elegy*, for example, Vance seems intent on identifying the family and community traits that can explain the cycles of addiction and abuse that he managed to escape. But Vance's up-by-the-bootstraps tale oddly ignores the larger social and economic forces around his family and instead emphasizes personal character flaws.

At the ReSource, we see these attitudes in the social media responses to many of our stories. Comments on stories about black lung disease or poor access to drinking water are frequently peppered with some version of how the people deserved what had befallen them. *Have you seen how they vote, what they eat? Have you heard how they talk?*

It's a bipartisan brand of disdain, coming from both the left and right. Shortly after Trump's election, Markos Moulitsas, founder of the liberal blog *Daily Kos*, wrote a post titled "Be happy for coal miners losing their health insurance. They're getting exactly what they voted for."[11]

Sure, Moulitsas wrote, it was bad that thousands of miners might soon lose health and retirement benefits. "But how sorry should we be for this crowd?" he asked, when they voted heavily for Trump.

From the right, Kevin D. Williamson's essay in the *National Review*, "The White Ghetto," provides an especially noxious example of this thinking. Williamson used a road trip through eastern Kentucky and a few thousand colorful and insulting words to pose the question "Why not just leave?"

"Those who have the required work skills, the academic ability, or the simple desperate native enterprising grit to do so get the hell out as fast as they can," he wrote.[12]

Many do leave, of course. Out-migration from Appalachia is nearly as old as the region itself. But many can't leave when economic conditions shift. Family obligations or falling home prices limit the ability to move to where the jobs are. In an era of wage stagnation and the rising cost of living in urban areas, there is also little incentive to move for a low-paying job in a high-cost city.

For many others, the deep-rooted traditions, natural beauty of the land, and sense of place are strong incentives to stay. Hard as it may be for Williamson and his ilk to grasp, many people actually *like* living in the place where they're from, where generations of family lived, loved, worked, played, and are now buried. They take seriously the duty to honor a place's past and care deeply about their community's future. That's just one of many ways the Appalachian experience challenges American assumptions about progress.

There is also a hidden cost inherent in the assumption of mobility, the belief that people will always simply move to find new economic opportunity. The places and people left behind are then increasingly viewed as unworthy of investment and attention, as disposable.

That may work out well for the larger society, so long as the "disposable" place is small and the people there have limited power. But what happens when more places and more people become disposable? What happens when the Appalachian experience becomes the more common American one?

Consider the implications of rapid advancements in technologies such as artificial intelligence, advanced robotics, and driverless vehicles. We don't yet know how these technologies will affect employment, but recent work from the Brookings Institution suggests that if you drive for a living, work in manufacturing, enter data or keep the books at an office, cook or serve food, or send products down a belt at an Amazon "fulfillment center," it is quite possible that the rapidly approaching wave of technological change will affect your job, your family, your community.[13]

In other words, the next "hillbilly" could just as easily be you. Appalachia's experience with economic dislocation and social ills could soon be a much more widespread phenomenon.

Or consider the origin and spread of the opioid crisis. Much of the country is just waking up to the full extent of the epidemic, which now claims more American lives than car crashes. Appalachians, however, have had a two-decade preview of this disaster.

The addiction and overdose rates here soared in the early 2000s as painkiller prescriptions poured into small towns. People in hardworking yet distressed towns were primed for addiction by a potent mix: bodies battered by physical labor and spirits stifled by economic hopelessness.

Add to that the predatory marketing of Purdue Pharma and other opioid makers and distributors, and soon the region was awash in "pill mills" pumping out pain medicine. OxyContin paved the way for cheap heroin by providing a ready customer base when authorities finally cracked down on pill mills. Deadlier synthetic opioids such as fentanyl followed, creating what health researchers call a "triple-wave crisis."

As bad as the opioid crisis is around the country, it is worse here. Huntington, West Virginia, where President Trump held some of his rallies in the state, had the nation's highest death rate from synthetic opioids in 2017.[14] In that same year, West Virginia had the nation's highest rate of fatal drug overdoses, with 57.8 deaths per 100,000 people—nearly three times the national average. Ohio had the second-highest rate. Kentucky was fifth highest.[15]

In the three states combined, roughly twenty people died from overdose each day in 2017. That's six hundred people each month, and more than 7,200 in a year. These three states represented just 6 percent of the country's total population but accounted for about 10 percent of the nation's opioid overdose deaths.

Health officials have a term for deaths from drug overdose, alcohol, and suicide: "diseases of despair." It's an evocative phrase that aptly connects the palpable sense of hopelessness in many hard-hit communities to the concrete statistics of mortality.

Through the early 2000s, OxyContin was known as "hillbilly heroin." But the crisis crept out of central Appalachia, into struggling former steel mill and manufacturing towns of the Midwest, and beyond.

Today, diseases of despair that have long plagued Appalachians are so common in other regions that health researchers say that the overall mortality rate is climbing among people in the prime of life. The collective toll is now bending the curve of life expectancy downward, not just for Appalachia but for the country as a whole.[16]

The ways that Appalachian communities respond to this epidemic also, by necessity, reveal how the crisis is tied to economic distress and the fraying of the social fabric. Recovery from mass addiction will rely on broader economic recovery that truly supports community.

MORE PARTS OF THE country are also now experiencing the sort of concentrated economic disparity that has long defined Appalachia, and current research shows a correlation between high inequality and voter support for authoritarian candidates.

In October 2019, the Boston Federal Reserve Bank arranged a conference titled "A House Divided."[17] Some of the nation's leading economists argued that geographic disparities in economic well-being required a new set of policy approaches. Lawrence Summers, former president of Harvard University and director of the National Economic Council under President Obama, pointed out the problems in coal country and linked them to similar phenomena in regions with wealth disparities not just around the country but around the world.

"It is the disaffection of distant non-cosmopolitans who live away from major prospering capital cities that is the source of populist nationalism, anti-internationalism, reduced global cooperation," Summers said, listing Trumpism in the United States, Brexit in the UK, and the rise of authoritarianism in Eastern Europe, India, and Turkey as examples of conditions driving "increased incentives certainly to trade wars, and possibly conflicts going well beyond trade wars."

Political scientists Pippa Norris and Ronald Inglehart write about the "existential insecurity" that arises when parts of the country are left behind: "The economic stagnation and rising inequality of recent decades have led to increasing support for authoritarian, xenophobic political candidates."[18]

Sasha Polakow-Suransky, who wrote about anti-immigrant politics in *Go Back to Where You Came From*, warned that democracies "contain the seeds of their own destruction."[19] It's a notion that's been around since Plato first warned about the corrosive effects of inequality on democracy, when the *demos* split too sharply into haves and have-nots.

In April 2017, the eastern Kentucky town of Pikeville served as a testing ground for those ideas, and the extent to which extremism could attract a broader following in a struggling region.

The Traditionalist Worker Party, at the time led by a Maryland native transplanted to southern Indiana named Matthew Heimbach, announced plans for a rally in the town along with other groups, including the League of the South. Both the League and Traditionalist Workers have been identified by the Southern Poverty Law Center as hate groups, and both advanced an unapologetically racist rationale and remedy for the area's economic malaise.

Heimbach saw the area as fertile ground for his message of "standing up for white working families." Those in the area who still bothered to vote—as fewer than half the eligible residents in many counties in the area did in 2016—voted overwhelmingly for Donald Trump, something the white nationalists took as a key indicator of a receptive audience.

The white nationalists, about 150 of them, marched in Pikeville, but Pikeville largely looked the other way. Most local shops closed for the day, and while about 200 counter-demonstrators turned out to protest, most local people simply ignored the whole spectacle.

However, the Pikeville rally was just one of many throughout the region that summer and fall, part of a national wave of events that we now understand were a prelude to the mayhem and hatred that erupted a year later in Charlottesville, Virginia.

James Alex Fields Jr., the man who drove a car into a crowd in Charlottesville, killing one demonstrator and injuring dozens more, grew up in Kentucky and Ohio. On YouTube, you can watch a video of a group of white nationalists openly recruiting on a northern Kentucky street corner just a few miles from where Fields was attending high school at the time.

Many scholars link the appeal of authoritarianism and extremism to the disaffection of the working class, the decline of rural communities and the attendant addiction epidemic, and the growing geographic disparities in both wealth and health. All of these hit hardest and earliest in Appalachia, and all are now full-blown front-and-center crises for the nation as a whole.

These are no longer just Appalachian problems; they are American problems. Welcome to Appalach-America.

"I COINED THE PHRASE as long ago as the 1980s," John Gaventa said, "what we call the 'Appalachian-ization of America.'"

The clunky phrase fit what Gaventa, who is now director of research at the Institute of Development Studies at the University of Sussex, was beginning to see take shape forty years ago. The lost jobs and opportunity, declining social capital, and decaying infrastructure associated with Appalachia were becoming more common across parts of rural America.

Several historians who study Appalachia have since made a similar argument that the region is more a national bellwether than a backwater.

The historian John Alexander Williams wrote in *Appalachia: A History* that for much of the twentieth century the Appalachian question was about why the region had failed to keep up with the rest of the country in material measures. But today, Williams writes, Appalachia poses a different question: "It is reasonable to ask whether Appalachia may have led the nation, not lagged behind, into a future whose outline is only now just coming into view."[20]

Historian Ronald Eller reaches a similar conclusion in his history of Appalachia in the late twentieth century, *Uneven Ground.* Appalachia, he writes, "was no longer the other America. It *was* America, and the region's uncertain destiny stood as a warning to the rest of the nation."[21]

Appalachia is on the leading edge of many of America's major challenges: inequality, addiction, and the complexities of the clean energy transition necessary to forestall the worst of climate change. As resilient Appalachian communities respond to those challenges, they are attempting to build a different future for themselves and their communities. As both Gaventa and Eller see it, the work taking place in these communities holds the promise of elegant solutions that can address many problems at once, not just for the forgotten of coal country but for the country as a whole.

In small cities and towns where coal employment and revenue are disappearing, people are organizing to develop a more diverse and sustainable economic base, from promising new agriculture, from outdoor recreation, and from the region's rich arts and culture.

Public school leaders are also pooling resources to use the schools as a catalyst for change. Teachers and administrators know they must prepare students for a radically different world than the one their parents and grandparents knew.

In the heart of eastern Kentucky's coal country, twenty-two school districts serve some of the most rural, rugged country in Appalachia, towns and counties struggling with some of the country's most profound economic and public health challenges. But by working together, these schools found ways to innovate in classrooms and maybe help the region find a new path forward.

"We are really ambitious," Jeff Hawkins said. Hawkins leads the Kentucky Valley Educational Cooperative, or KVEC. The cooperative started with humble goals around 1970, he explained, as a way to provide driver's education courses and purchase school supplies in bulk.[22] But over time the cooperative expanded to teacher training and a wholesale reinvention of the classroom experience. KVEC schools emphasize personalized learning, team projects, and an entrepreneurial attitude that Hawkins thinks can make a difference in an area in need of change. "What we believe is that our K-through-twelve classes can serve as catalytic drivers to reinvent communities where we live."

Students have been inventing new products, building tiny houses, racing drones, and coding software. Bill Gates and Mark Zuckerberg have both visited and come away impressed.

In one hands-on technology classroom at Belfry High School in Pike County, freshman Jacob Bowman and his team of students experimented with alternative energy sources. "People would be surprised by this from what their stereotype for people around here is," he said. "Literally, we're proving their stereotypes wrong."

Chuck Fluharty calls the KVEC schools one of the brightest spots in Central Appalachia. Fluharty directs the Rural Policy Research Institute at the University of Iowa, where he has worked with communities dealing with economic change, from Missouri's farms to Minnesota's iron ore range. Fluharty said the situation in Appalachian coal country is among the toughest.

"It's called the resource curse in economics," Fluharty said. "When you have a company town, what tends to happen over time is you crowd out the potential of other industry to make a case for their future."

Jobs in the mines and businesses supporting them took up most of the labor supply and capital, and little effort went into diversifying the economy or training the workforce for anything else.

In most regions that rely on resource extraction, Fluharty said, change comes gradually as an industry lessens over time and decision-makers look at other options.

"In Kentucky this hit almost all at once," he said. Fluharty said initiatives like KVEC are among the best options to help turn the corner. But he and the cooperative's organizers are also aware of how precarious the project is.

Much of the work happening in the schools is supported by a federal education grant. Without it, inequities in the state's education funding system and the declining tax revenue base would make it difficult, if not impossible, to continue to offer the programs.

The same pattern holds true for many other promising projects aimed at retraining workers and reinventing local economies around the region, which often depend on time-limited grants.

The Appalachian Regional Commission is investing hundreds of millions in such projects through a series of grants aimed at communities hardest hit by the decline in the coal industry. But expert observers say those investments are woefully short of the scale needed to meet the region's enormous challenges. Much of Appalachia needs sustained, large-scale investment in education, health care, and infrastructure to heal the wounds inflicted by a century of resource extraction and create a new economy in a region long stunted by the resource curse.

That sort of investment will require political leadership informed by a clear-eyed assessment of the challenges ahead, something that is largely missing from much of the political rhetoric in the region. Politicians who rail against a "war on coal" and promise voters a "coal comeback" are not inclined to accept the overwhelming evidence of the industry's decline, the real economic factors driving that decline, or the real need to reduce emissions that threaten the stability of our climate system.

But the longer these leaders avoid the harsh realities, the harder they make it for the communities they were elected to serve. That message comes through in expert analyses of the coal industry's future and fiscal implications for mining towns.

"While some politicians in coal-reliant areas may claim to have a path to bringing coal back," the authors of a Brookings Institution report write, "such bluster is irresponsible given the robust negative projections for the industry."[23]

The outcome will likely have effects far beyond the rural towns and rugged hills of Appalachia. We already see evidence that the country suffers when it allows a region to fall. Yet we lack any comprehensive strategy for an economic transition, let alone one that makes whole the places left behind. Many community leaders here recognize this, even if many elected leaders will not. They are making the argument that Appalachia can not only heal itself; if supported, it can share that success with other American communities that have fallen behind.

2.
Bloody Harlan County: Then and Now

CURTIS CRESS SAT in the gravel beside a railroad track in Harlan County, Kentucky. Tall and thin, with a long, black beard, Cress is every bit the coal miner. Or he was, until a few days earlier.

"It's part of my heritage, you know? My dad and papaws had always done it," he said. "And I'm proud of that heritage."

Cress had been at these railroad tracks for days, with little sleep. Not far down the rails sat a row of hopper cars filled with coal from his former employer, Blackjewel, which had been the nation's sixth largest coal mining company.

In the span of a month, Cress and his fellow miners had gone from getting coal out of the ground to stopping that coal in its tracks. Blackjewel's chaotic bankruptcy filing on July 1, 2019,[1] left Cress and more than a thousand other Appalachian miners with bounced checks and unpaid bills, and largely in the dark about their future.[2]

"My family's hungry, and I'm gonna do whatever it takes to feed them," Blackjewel miner Bobby Sexton said. "We want answers, we want our money, we want to get paid."

Blackjewel employed some 1,100 miners in Kentucky, Virginia, and

The first few Blackjewel Coal miners who took to the railroad tracks in Harlan County, Kentucky, in the morning fog on the first full day of the protest that would stretch on for nearly three months. The men were blockading a trainload of coal they had mined but had not been paid for.

West Virginia and nearly another 600 at large surface mines the company had recently purchased in Wyoming's Powder River Basin.

Bankruptcies have become common in coal country, with major producers such as Peabody Energy and Arch Coal among the dozens of companies seeking protection to undergo some form of restructuring in the past decade. Blackjewel is among roughly a dozen mining companies to go under since President Trump took office vowing to bring coal back. Most of those companies have continued operations. In fact, as much as 70 percent of the coal mined in the United States today comes from companies that have gone through bankruptcy.

But Blackjewel's bankruptcy was exceptional for its speed and chaos. The company owed millions of dollars to creditors and tens of millions more to the government in taxes, unpaid fines for safety and environmental violations, and mineral royalties. And then, of course, there were the workers.

Many Blackjewel miners learned from banks that their paychecks were bouncing or being "clawed back" after deposit. Days turned into weeks, and the miners had no way to know if they still had jobs or health insurance or access to their retirement savings. In a federal bankruptcy court in West Virginia, Judge Frank Volk expressed sympathy.

"The court is concerned about the employees," Volk said during a July 19 hearing. "Where do they fall in the scheme in respect to recoveries in this case?" But that question remained unanswered for weeks.

On July 29, five miners saw an opportunity. A train full of coal was leaving a Blackjewel loading facility in Harlan County. Word spread via social media and phone, and five men clambered onto the railroad tracks to block the train.[3]

"If they can move this train, they can give us our money!" miner Shane Smith said.

The group grew to nine. Police asked them to clear the tracks, but the miners simply moved to a different spot on the rails and stood their ground. Curtis Cress's wife, Felicia, used a black marker and a cardboard pizza box to fashion a protest sign: "No Pay, We Stay."

"We're gonna make a stand," Bobby Sexton said. "I don't know if I'll go home if they don't pay us. I'll sit here until . . ." He thought for a moment: "Until whenever." The following foggy morning the miners were still on the tracks, holding off the trainload of coal.

Miners directed their ire at Blackjewel's CEO, Jeff Hoops. Hoops began his career in coal at age seventeen and worked his way to an executive position with Arch Coal, one of the country's largest mining companies, before starting his own companies in the late 1990s, earning millions.

His Hoops Family Foundation is known for philanthropy in the area. The children's wing at Cabell Huntington Hospital, in Huntington, West Virginia, bears the Hoops name, as do sports facilities at colleges and universities around the state. Hoops and his wife, Patricia, also support Christian missionary work in India and other parts of the developing world.

But Hoops's mining businesses have long been controversial, with a trail of unpaid fines for environmental damages and work safety violations. An investigation by the ReSource found that Hoops's companies were responsible for more than $926,000 in delinquent mine safety fines from the federal Mine Safety and Health Administration.

And yet Hoops was able to purchase struggling mines from other companies over the objections of citizen watchdog groups.

Shortly after the company filed for bankruptcy, Hoops sent an all-staff email to Blackjewel employees. He wrote that in the days leading up to the filing, he had personally tried to loan the company more money but was advised by a financier not to do so.

"No one is hurting more than me over what has occurred," Hoops wrote.

When a ReSource reporter managed to reach Hoops by phone during the miners' protest, he said he was also bothered by the situation with the unpaid miners.

"I'm as frustrated as they are," he said. "I have no idea what's going on there. I'm really sorry that it's reached this point."

That did not garner much sympathy from the miners in Harlan County. A popular T-shirt started to appear among those standing vigil on the tracks. It showed a Calvin-style cartoon character urinating on the name "Jeff Hoops."

Within days, the ragtag group of protesters had grown to a full-fledged protest camp. A local funeral home donated some tents to provide some respite from the ruthless July heat; the supportive local government provided porta-potties and some lighting, as well as a solar-powered road sign urging motorists to slow down as they approached the protest.

And two local activists arrived, volunteering to take on some of the day-to-day logistics of running the camp.

"At first we didn't really know who they were, but we got used to them," said Stacy Rowe, a miner's wife and one of the most dedicated protesters.

The new arrivals were transgender anarchists. With their gender nonconformity and vocabulary of left-wing protest, the pair stood out in the blossoming network of tents and canopies beside the railroad. As national and even international news outlets picked up the story, they also got a glimpse of a different kind of Appalachian than they'd expected.

The miners gave the anarchists control over how donations should be used, and the two became unofficial babysitters of the protest's many children. At night, after the journalists had gone, coal miners and trans activists sat on the railroad tracks together, gazing into the fire and up at the stars, and talked about where they agreed and where they didn't on the social issues that are said to divide us.

But under it all, the suffering continued.

"We're suffering, our kids are suffering, water's getting cut off," Austin Watts said. "As long as I gotta stay here, I'll stay."

Arnold Shepherd, a miner from Leslie County, Kentucky, was among those missing pay. Taking in the scene at the growing protest, he was reminded of an earlier period in Harlan County history.

"This thing here, it puts you in mind of Bloody Harlan, back years ago," Shepherd said.

Bloody Harlan. The name comes from the decades-long and often violent struggle between coal companies and workers seeking better treatment and a union—something the Blackjewel miners no longer had.

"People who risk themselves, that is what has resonance to a long body of history," labor historian Dr. Rosemary Feurer said. An associate professor at Northern Illinois University, Feurer studies and writes about labor conflict.[4] She argued that when the Blackjewel miners put their bodies on those tracks, they were connecting to that region's tradition of resistance.

"You have to look at Bloody Harlan in a long history of a bloody coal industry," she said. And she's not just talking about the blood shed in labor conflicts, such as the mine wars that roiled Appalachia in the early part of the twentieth century. Rather, she refers to the total costs that the mining industry has consistently pushed onto the workers and the environment.

The combined death toll over the past century from explosions, cave-ins, and other disasters, and especially the slow-rolling disaster of black lung disease, runs into the hundreds of thousands. "It's more than most wars," Feurer said. "What the miners were saying is, we can't be basically just extraction engines and robots and tools left to die."

The United Mine Workers of America had their first success organizing coalfields to the north of Kentucky around the turn of the twentieth century, negotiating for wage increases, an eight-hour workday, and standard measurements for coal. Mine operators pushed back by increasing production in places like southern West Virginia and eastern Kentucky, where the companies enjoyed friendly local governments and near total domination over life in coal camp communities.

"Harlan is one of the locations used to undercut wage stability for the rest of the country," Feurer said. Harlan miners started to organize in the 1920s, a struggle that culminated in a long and violent strike in 1931 that gave rise to the moniker "Bloody Harlan."

The operators' local ally was Sheriff John "J. H." Blair, whose tyrannical rule inspired Florence Reese, a union organizer and the wife of a miner, to give the labor movement one of its great anthems, "Which Side Are You On?"

They say in Harlan County
There are no neutrals there
You'll either be a union man
Or a thug for J. H. Blair.

In that especially brutal period in the early days of the Depression, striking miners were beaten, shot, blacklisted, and evicted from coal company housing. Places where miners met to organize were dynamited.

In the fall of 1931, the writers Theodore Dreiser, John Dos Passos, and Sherwood Anderson formed a committee to visit Harlan County, take testimony from miners, and witness conditions in the coal camps. The visit resulted in a book, *Harlan Miners Speak.*

Dreiser, a committed socialist, wrote that what was happening in Harlan was "a very remarkable struggle of the American worker against the usual combination of power and wealth in America."

The miners, he said, were up against not only the coal companies but other local institutions as well. "The small town bankers, grocers, editors, and lawyers, the police, the sheriff . . . were all apparently subservient to the money and corporate masters of the area."[5]

Dreiser reflected on the mindset of the local power structure that led so many people of modest means to identify more strongly with distant, wealthy elites than with their neighboring workers.

"Possibly, this springs from the asinine notion in America that everyone has an equal opportunity to become a money master, a Morgan or a Rockefeller," Dreiser wrote. "The data concerning America's economic life today show that no more than 350 families control 95 percent of the wealth of the country."

OF COURSE, this data is nearly identical to what we have today. The country's richest three people, Jeff Bezos, Warren Buffett, and Bill Gates, represent more wealth than do the roughly 160 million people in the lower half of the country's income scale. Just three families in the United States today have an estimated combined $348.7 billion in wealth. That is *4 million times* more than the wealth of an average American family.[6]

And while there are no Harlan miners today being shot, beaten, or dynamited, some of the testimony in *Harlan Miners Speak* could just as easily have come from one of today's Blackjewel miners who took to the railroad tracks in protest.

One coal camp resident Dos Passos and Dreiser heard from went by the name Aunt Molly Jackson. Her full name was Mary Magdalene Garland Stewart Jackson Stamos. A midwife, Jackson said she had delivered more than eight hundred babies. She was also a folk singer, and part of her testimony came in a song, one of many she would later record as a folk artist, called "Kentucky Miner's Wife (Ragged Hungry Blues)." The chorus went:

Listen, friends and comrades,
Please take a friend's advice,
Don't load no more o' that dirty coal,
Till you get a living price.

Conflict broke out again in Harlan County in the 1970s. Two miners were shot and one died in a strike that lasted over a year before the union won a new contract. But beginning in the 1980s, industry practices began to shift toward far more automation and large-scale surface mining, triggering a decline in hiring that continues today.

The union's share of employment in coal country declined even faster. Government data show that by 2017 only about 6,800 Appalachian miners were union members. The decline was sharpest in the central Appalachian coalfields. In West Virginia, the percentage of mine workers in unions dropped from 56 percent to 26 percent over twenty years. In that same period, the percentage of Kentucky miners in the union dropped from 12 percent to less than 1 percent.

Harlan County, which so famously bled for its union, now has no working union miners. By the time the Blackjewel miners took to the tracks, "Which side are you on?" was a moot question. There was no other side. There was simply what the company offered or what could be wrung from a bankruptcy court.

"I think it's tragic that there are no active union mines in Kentucky," Cecil Roberts said from his office at the UMWA headquarters in Virginia. He was considering the Blackjewel miners and what their predicament said about the mining industry. "We've really fallen a great distance here when workers have to block a train to get the wages they've already earned."

Roberts, a native of Cabin Creek, West Virginia, has been the UMWA's president since 1995. Only one person has served longer in that post: the legendary John L. Lewis. But while Lewis's tenure saw the heyday of union numbers and power, Roberts's time coincides roughly with the declines in membership.

A Vietnam veteran, Roberts went to work in the mines after leaving the army and joined the movement to reform the UMWA, which was emerging from a period of deep corruption and violent infighting. Onstage at a rally, Roberts will often shout himself hoarse with stemwinder speeches. But in interviews he is soft-spoken, reflective. He is clearly pained by the current state of his industry and the region where he grew up.

"I would argue that this might be the most challenging time not only for coal miners but for people in Appalachia because of the severe decline in coal and the jobs that coal supported," he said. In his old haunts in southern West Virginia, he said, he sees schools that relied on coal revenues cutting back, hospitals closing, and lifelong residents wrestling with how long they can stay as home prices dwindle. "Probably the only time in our history that was anywhere near this bad may have been the Great Depression."

Roberts rejected the rhetoric from the coal industry that the Trump administration is bringing coal back.

"No one's saved the coal industry. The coal industry isn't back."

Instead he sees a continuing wave of coal company bankruptcies and "restructuring," further chipping away at both the wages of current miners and the pensions of retirees.

"Why should workers stand in line last? Why should it be beneficial to a CEO or CFO to file bankruptcy? They ran the company into the ground, they get rich, the workers lose their health care, or lose their jobs, or lose their pensions," he said. "That needs to be dealt with."

At the time of our interview, Roberts worried that the UMWA's pension plan couldn't withstand the strain of more company bankruptcies unless Congress intervened to prop up the miners' plan and others like it, known as multiemployer pension plans. As more coal companies go under, the ones left standing are responsible for covering those in "orphaned" company plans.

"We have over eighty thousand people who are currently drawing a pension, and probably another ten thousand or more people out there who have not yet retired but have earned a pension," he said. "It's not looking very bright right now. People are terrified."

The previous summer, Roberts took to the stage in a plaza in downtown Columbus, Ohio, leading a crowd of thousands of union workers and retirees in a chant: "Fix it!" This was not the quiet, reflective Roberts. This was the shouting, fist-shaking Roberts. "When the people get to marching, the politicians get to listening!" Roberts roared.

Nearby, lawmakers were preparing for a field hearing of a joint select congressional committee assigned to address the solvency threats to multiemployer pension plans.

Retired Kentucky coal miner Virgil Stanley at a UMWA rally for miners' health benefits and pensions. Stanley worked for more than twenty years for Peabody Energy, which declared bankruptcy in 2016.

The UMWA wasn't the only union plan in trouble. Teamsters, ironworkers, carpenters, and others fear their pensions are shaky at best. In the hearing, lawmakers learned of the likely dire effects if major pension plans fail—not just for the affected industries but for the larger economy.

"I see the light in the tunnel," Senator Joe Manchin, a West Virginia Democrat on the panel, said. "And it is sure as hell not the daylight on the other side. I see this train wreck coming."

Senator Rob Portman, Republican from Ohio, warned that a "wave of bankruptcy has the potential to create an economic contagion effect," and if enough of the larger plans become insolvent that could put the federal Pension Benefit Guaranty Corporation at risk as well.

"In other words, it would spread around our economy," Portman said.

But the panel also heard from business owners frustrated that they were saddled with pension costs for workers from other long-gone companies. Conservative policy groups, such as the Heritage Foundation, argued that congressional action would amount to a bailout. Portman wondered aloud how much taxpayers should pitch in when "ninety-nine percent of the taxpayers who are going to be asked to contribute" have no stake in the affected plans.

The committee listened. It mulled. It issued warnings. But despite pending legislation with bipartisan support to address the pension shortfalls, it did not act.

The UMWA has been ringing the alarm on pension and health benefit risks for years. Busloads of union retirees don matching camo-patterned T-shirts and UMWA ballcaps and make trips from their small coalfield towns to rally in Columbus, in St. Louis, in Washington, DC.

After years of seeing bipartisan bills to support pensions languish in Senate committees, the union finally got a victory as 2019 came to a close. The Senate majority leader, Mitch McConnell of Kentucky, agreed to a bill that would redirect some money from a fund for cleaning up abandoned mine lands and put those funds toward supporting miners' pensions and health benefits. Once again, the experience in Appalachian coal country may be foreshadowing what's to come for Americans elsewhere. Now the question is whether other industries with shaky pension plans will also require federal intervention.

ON AUGUST 5, 2019, about fifty Blackjewel miners and their supporters loaded buses of their own for the trip from the Harlan railroad tracks to the courtroom in Charleston, West Virginia, where a bankruptcy judge was considering bids for what was left of Blackjewel and the competing interests who were owed money. The miners filed in wearing lime-green T-shirts that read "Harlan County Strong" and "Pay Miners First and Lawyers Last."

"I commend members of the mining profession who joined us," Judge Volk said. "You can make a very powerful statement without saying anything at all."

But as the miners listened quietly to the complexities of the bankruptcy, it became clear that the lawyers would most definitely not be the last.

Potential purchasers were ready to buy up Blackjewel properties, but it was clear the sales would not generate enough to cover more than a fraction of the company's massive outstanding debts. An attorney representing Blackjewel argued that most of the coal the miners were blocking had already been purchased by another party and therefore should be allowed to move. An attorney for Caterpillar, the heavy equipment company, told the court the company is owed more than $26 million for equipment in Appalachia and expressed concern that there would not be enough to pay that debt after sales are completed. Several surety bond representatives told the court all cash earned through the sales should be set aside until Blackjewel made clear just how much it owed for things like reclamation obligations to cover the costs of environmental damage from surface mining.

Blackjewel's bankruptcy has been messier than most. But Clark

Williams-Derry, an analyst with the Institute for Energy Economics and Financial Analysis, said it could be a harbinger of more to come.

"We're sort of in the early stages of the endgame, I would say, of the coal economy," he said.

Williams-Derry worries that, as fewer companies remain, the costs of worker pensions, land reclamation, and other debts may well be passed on to taxpayers or left unpaid altogether.

"We're in uncharted territory," he said. "We don't really know what happens when the industry is shrinking so rapidly that we see mines just simply abandoned."

BLACKJEWEL'S BRIEF CORPORATE LIFE tells us a lot about how the coal industry uses bankruptcy to avoid its legacy costs—the costs for pensions and health benefits for workers and the costs to repair damaged lands and waterways near mines.

Much of what would become Blackjewel once belonged to a mining company called Alpha Natural Resources. Alpha had taken over several of the mines once operated by Massey Energy, the mining company made infamous by the Upper Big Branch mining disaster that killed twenty-nine miners in 2010.

Alpha pledged to turn things around and "run right" with attention to safety. But by August of 2015 Alpha filed for bankruptcy. The company owed more than $2 billion in pensions and health-care coverage for miners, but it persuaded a Virginia bankruptcy court to discharge much of those obligations. As Joshua Macey and Jackson Salovaara explain in the *Stanford Law Review*, that meant some ten thousand current or retired miners lost their health-care benefits.[7]

But Alpha needed to shed more debt to remain viable. Much more. The company split in two. A new company emerged: Contura—a name as sleek as a new model of sedan. Contura effectively sped away from its old debts, which were largely left in the old company, Alpha.

Alpha and Contura both sold off some of the mines that had the highest obligations to workers and the highest costs for environmental restoration. But who would take on properties burdened with that sort of debt?

Alpha found a willing taker in Jeff Hoops. Some Alpha properties became part of Hoops-owned companies Lexington Coal, Revelation Energy, and Blackjewel.

"This series of reorganizations effectively shielded Alpha's profitable mines from half a billion dollars' worth of environmental liabilities," Macey and Salovaara wrote.

With these nettlesome debts behind it, Alpha and Contura happily reunited. At a March 2017 event at the Trump Mar-a-Lago resort, Alpha was recognized as "reorganization of the year" by M&A Advisors, a group that recognizes "top performers" in mergers, acquisitions, and turnarounds.

Alpha was following a well-trod path for coal companies dealing with rising debts amid a downturn in their industry. Macey and Salovaara estimate that from 2012 to 2017, four of the country's biggest coal companies "succeeded in shedding" almost $5.2 billion in costs owed for worker benefits, retiree pensions, and environmental liabilities. Even though about a fifth of all the companies' liabilities arose from obligations under federal law, all were "shed" under the watchful eye of bankruptcy judges.

As Macey and Salovaara point out, this means that about 20 percent of debts "shed" were not business debts "but rather liabilities under federal laws intended to force companies to mitigate environmental damage and to honor pension and health care obligations."

It's a funny term, "shedding obligations." Dogs shed hair; trees shed leaves. But how does a company "shed" something like its obligations to a retired worker or the reclamation of hills left barren and denuded by strip-mining?

In an interview, Macey, then a visiting assistant professor at Cornell University, explained that part of the answer lies in the bankruptcy courts' inherent desire to have a troubled company emerge intact. That's presumed to be better for employees, communities, and creditors—including the states, which are often looking at taking on millions of dollars in reclamation work if a company dissolves.

"Most bankruptcy judges do not want to insist on liquidation," which would end employment and tax revenue and force immediate reclamation of mine lands. Coal companies take advantage of that, he said, to negotiate reductions in debt obligations.

The other "shedding" comes when a company spins off its most troubled assets. In Alpha's case, those debts were shed with help from Jeff Hoops.

"Hoops's strategy was to find ways to get paid to off-load the most troubled assets," Macey said.

Hoops didn't buy the Alpha mines, exactly. Alpha paid him to take on properties laden with obligations for worker benefits and environmental cleanup. This happened even though Hoops had a history of taking on troubled mines, getting large sums from the companies that wanted to be rid of them, and then doing little to resolve those problems.

"There was no way that company was going to be profitable," Macey said of Blackjewel. But because these are private companies funded via privately held debt, Hoops could pay himself. "Hoops treated these as his personal piggy bank."

EARLY IN BLACKJEWEL'S BANKRUPTCY, Jeff Hoops was ousted. Creditors demanded that neither Hoops nor his family would be authorized to conduct business on behalf of the company.

Hoops and his wife, Patricia, are turning their attention to other projects, like developing a massive resort hotel and spa in his hometown of Milton, West Virginia. Hoops told the *Charleston Gazette-Mail* the resort's name is a play on his wife's: the Grand Patrician.[8]

According to the Grand Patrician's website, the multimillion-dollar, 189-acre resort will have a hundred-room hotel, miles of equestrian trails, and four baseball fields designed as replicas of famous venues like Yankee Stadium and Fenway Park. A golf course will be modeled after famous PGA tour holes at Pebble Beach and Augusta. A 3,500-seat replica of the Roman Colosseum will host live theatrical productions every weekend.

The Roman theme extends to a wedding chapel, where "a gilded foyer leads into ornate arched ceilings," the website said. "For today's couples, The Grand Patrician Resort represents the dream location to begin their new life together!"

A spokesperson for the resort's major financier, Clearwater Investment Holdings, told the *Huntington Herald-Dispatch* that the Grand Patrician is "still a go" and will continue uninterrupted by the Blackjewel bankruptcy.[9]

ON THE TRACKS in Harlan County, the miners listened in via a conference line as another marathon bankruptcy hearing brought mixed news.[10] The auction of Blackjewel properties attracted enough buyers to generate money to go toward some of the wages owed, and lawyers representing the miners were able to win some concessions from other Blackjewel creditors.

Still, when attorney Ned Pillersdorf addressed the protesting miners, he was clearly managing expectations.

"You know, I've told you, that bankruptcy is kind of like a funeral," he said. "Nobody leaves happy."

Kopper Glo, a Knoxville, Tennessee, mining company that purchased some of Blackjewel's Kentucky properties, has committed to pay $450,000 to cover miners' wages. That is expected to cover about 35 percent of the total amount owed to Blackjewel workers. Kopper Glo has also said it hopes to rehire many of Blackjewel's workers, though it has made no legal commitment to do so. Blackjewel miners worry Kopper Glo will pay less than Blackjewel did.

"I was a roof bolter; I made $25 an hour," said Shane Smith. "A belt man, they make $22. A different company comes in, what's to say everybody won't make $20?"

Kopper Glo said in a press release it has a plan to restart certain operations and "is confident this plan will bring jobs back to many of the former Blackjewel employees."

In their weeks spent occupying the train tracks, the Blackjewel miners had plenty of time to consider what their future holds. Do they return to work and hope their new employer doesn't meet the same fate as the last? Do they look for another job, knowing they may never make as much money as they did in the mines? Or do they try to retrain in a new industry?

"This ain't a game; we ain't a bunch of kids," said miner Caleb Blevins. "We're grown men with families. Around here in the Appalachian Mountains, this is all we got, the coal mines. We're too far in to try to go to college for twelve years. Our kids need us now, not in ten years."

Miner Tim Madden also just wanted to get back to business as usual. "I think if they'd roll up here and issue us all a check, I'd be out of here, end of story."

But Curtis Cress said he's done with the industry. "You never know from one day to the next if you're going to have a job," Cress said. "They'll get you used to making a whole lot of money and then take it away."

A father of four, Cress was at risk of losing his home. He feels hopeless about what comes next, both for him and for central Appalachia. He said he thinks his best bet is to find work in manufacturing. He hopes his kids leave the region when they're old enough.

The miners got another win later, when the US Department of Labor intervened in the bankruptcy, arguing that the load of coal the miners were blocking on the tracks should be considered "hot goods" in violation of fair labor standards, and should not be allowed to move or to be sold until there was compensation for the labor that produced it. But even with that action, the miners did not get full repayment.

After fifty-nine days on the tracks, the protest fizzled to an end. The miners needed to take new jobs, start classes, or move away from their coal-dependent communities.

Felicia Cress had been there with her husband, Curtis, since day one. "It was a bad situation that made us come together, stay there day and night, through the rain, through the blazing sun," she said. "We have new friendships, you know, we have a bond."

Their protest drew international attention, helped win miners a portion of their back pay, and highlighted the state's failure to collect bond payments from companies like Blackjewel, as the law requires. But at the end of it, the Cresses were still dealing with a bank threatening to foreclose on their home.

"This happened because we got shafted, which happens all the time," Felicia Cress said. "You got these rich people that shit on these poor people, and people just overlook it."

PROFILE:
Terry Steele

"EVERYTHING GOING ON now seems to be designed for division," Terry Steele said. Steele is talking about work and politics and how politicians talk about workers. He's heard a lot of it in his sixty-seven years in southern West Virginia, and he doesn't like much of what he hears lately.

"It's just a lot of bad propaganda," Steele said, "which is always well designed by people in power to convince poor people to kick some other poor people in the ass."

Steele estimates he has spent more than fifty thousand hours underground in his twenty-six years as a miner.

"A union miner!" he is quick to clarify. His local, United Mine Workers Local 1440, was once the largest in West Virginia with more than 1,200 members.[1]

Steele's the fourth generation in his family to mine coal. He grew up in "a little old town called Matewan."

Matewan—often called "Bloody Matewan," like Harlan County—is where miners and their hero, the town police chief Sid Hatfield, shot it out with coal company guards in 1920, leaving ten dead in the street. Hatfield himself was later gunned down on the courthouse steps in nearby Welch.

Steele's wife, Wilma, helps run the Mine Wars Museum in Matewan to keep that history alive. It's a busy time for the small museum. The year 2020 marks the centenary of the Matewan Massacre, and the following year, 2021, will mark one hundred years since another seminal yet overlooked event in the history of labor organizing in the coalfields—the Battle of Blair Mountain.

"There's been nothing quite like it in modern American history," labor historian James Green said. "It was the largest civil insurrection in the United States since the Civil War."

Green, who died in 2016, was interviewed in 2010 while working on what would be his last book, *The Devil Is Here in These Hills*, about Blair Mountain and the labor unrest in the coalfields in the early decades of the twentieth century.[2]

The union had successfully organized most coal operations in northern Appalachia, Green said, but southern West Virginia was nonunion and fiercely protected by coal operators, who often controlled the local political establishment. Mingo County, where Terry Steele grew up, was one example.

"Martial law had been declared in Mingo County, union organizers were put in jail, they were not allowed jury trials, no one was allowed to even read the newspaper in Mingo County," Green said.

In late August 1921, some ten thousand union coal miners armed themselves with hunting rifles and surplus World War I weapons to march from Kanawha County to Mingo County. To get there, the miners had to cross Blair Mountain, where coal operators had a mercenary force of their own, led by a sheriff named Don Chafin.

"Chafin and his men had fortified Blair Mountain with machine guns and their own army of over three thousand men. So it really was a full-scale battle," Green said.

The battle raged for days. Coal operators dropped crude bombs from biplanes—among the first aerial bombings of US civilians. It took federal troops to end the fighting. But maybe the most remarkable thing about the Battle of Blair Mountain is how few Americans have heard of it.

"I still don't think a lot of people know the history of the area," Steele said. "It wasn't taught in schools, and if it wasn't taught in homes, you'd have no idea how our union got started."

If it weren't for a small cadre of people dedicated to preservation, the history of Blair Mountain would have been buried—literally—a decade ago. The Arch Coal Company's Blair surface mine, a massive mountaintop removal operation, was blasting the nearby ridge, reducing it to rubble, and moving closer to the core of the site of the 1921 battle.

Amateur enthusiasts combed the ridge with maps and metal detectors, unearthing and documenting a trove of artifacts, including shell casings, earthworks, and bunkers. Meanwhile, allies petitioned state and federal agencies to win protection for Blair Mountain on the National Register of Historic Places.

In 2019, the Mine Wars Museum won a $30,000 grant from the National Endowment for the Humanities to plan its centennial project. The organizers are hoping that reviving interest in the region's labor history can foster cultural and historical tourism and "give a challenged community hope for the future through respect for the past," as the NEH news release put it.[3]

Even as Terry and Wilma Steele work to protect the union's history, they are witnessing its decline. Terry's once-mighty UMW Local 1440 still has some eight hundred members, but not one of them is still mining coal.

"We have nobody who's currently working in the mines; they're all retired miners," he said. "Most of them in their seventies, eighties. I'm a spring chicken in this place."

As he sees it, coal companies were effective at getting people to think that modern government regulation meant they didn't need unions or, worse, that the companies were a better friend to miners than the union was.

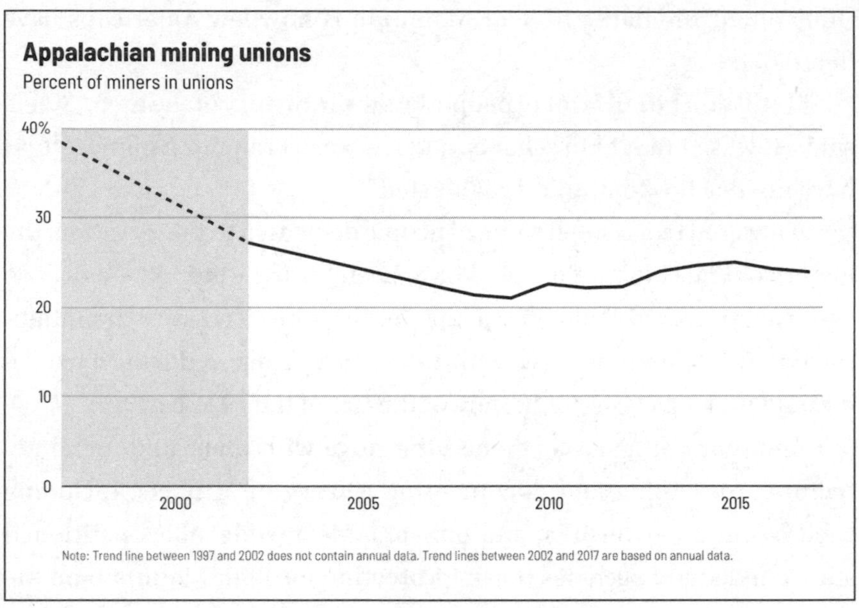

The coal associations of Kentucky and West Virginia ran one of the most successful marketing campaigns in the region. Their slogan, "Friends of Coal," graces billboards, license plates, ball caps, and T-shirts across Appalachian coal country.

"People danced a jig to Hank Williams Jr., saying unions was against the working man," Steele grumbled. For the uninitiated, during the height of the Reagan era, Williams sang:

The union's against the workers
Working against their will.[4]

Steele has still not forgiven Bocephus, nor the politicians of both parties who turned against labor starting in the 1980s.

"People are of the opinion now that unions are useless," he said. "And sad to say, too, they're gonna find out the hard way that they're not."

3.
Coshocton's Power Switch

JOE EGGLESTON SITS attentively behind a long plastic table inside a conference room at the Conesville power plant in Coshocton County, Ohio. Sporting a thick, dark beard and baseball hat, Eggleston, who has worked at the coal-fired power plant for twelve years, is studiously taking notes. His freshly updated résumé sits on the desk near his notebook.

It's just after 3:30 p.m. on the last Tuesday in April 2019. A sign over the clock reads, "If you change the way you look at things, the things you look at will change."

Things are certainly changing quickly for Eggleston and hundreds of others who work at the Conesville plant.

The previous fall, American Electric Power, one of the country's biggest coal-burning electric utilities, announced it was moving up the closure date for the generating units at Conesville by two years. The last unit was set to shutter in May 2020. Across the United States, coal plants are powering down.

According to the US Energy Information Administration, between 2007 and 2018, more than five hundred coal-fired generators, representing almost 22 percent of all coal-generated electricity capacity in the country, closed down.[1] Utilities have announced the retirement of at least 117 more coal units in the coming five years, according to a recent study by the Institute for Energy Economics and Financial Analysis.[2]

AEP executives have been signaling for years that the utility was on a path to greatly reduce its coal consumption because of abundant natural gas, declining electricity demand, and the improving economics of renewable energy sources. The shift from coal means cleaner air for those downwind of power plants, where particulate matter and other pollutants still take a terrible toll on public health despite improvements in emissions controls. The fuel switch is also helping to reduce greenhouse gas emissions from the electricity sector. But for each host community, the news of a plant closure comes as a blow.

Communities in the Ohio Valley will be hit especially hard. In addition to the Conesville closure, FirstEnergy Solutions Corporation is shuttering three other power plants: the Bruce Mansfield power plant in Beaver County, Pennsylvania; the W. H. Sammis power plant in Jefferson County, Ohio; and Pleasants power station in Pleasants County, West Virginia. And in Kentucky, the Tennessee Valley Authority shrugged off pressure from President Trump to keep burning coal at its once-massive facility in the town of Paradise. Instead, the TVA voted to shut down the last of its coal-burning units there after firing up a gleaming new natural gas generator on the site.

The Conesville plant has been a fixture in Coshocton County for sixty years, and working there was a lifelong dream for Eggleston. His father worked there for twenty-five years before him, and he's enjoyed his time at the plant.

"It's sad; you know, there's been a lot of generations that went through here," Eggleston says. "I hoped it would last longer."

But Eggleston isn't one to dwell on things he cannot change. He's taking advantage of every opportunity to prepare for life after the plant closes.

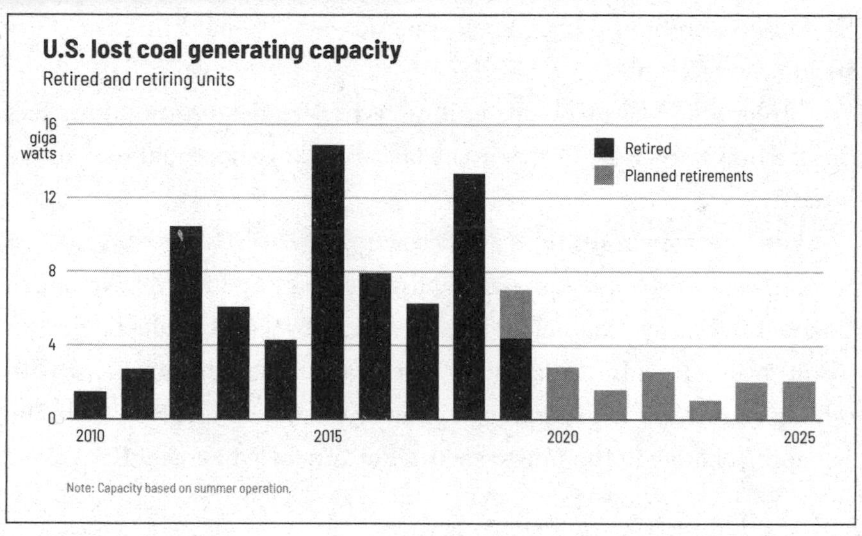

"It is what it is, and I'm just going to move forward," he says.

Today, that means sitting under the fluorescent lights in this conference room to hone a skill he has not had to use in years. A whiteboard in front of the room reads, "Interviewing: A Blueprint."

The Coshocton County chapter of OhioMeansJobs, a state-funded career counseling service, is hosting a series of résumé and job-interviewing classes at the plant. About a dozen participants came to an earlier résumé workshop, but today he's the lone participant for Interviewing 101.

After an hour-long lecture, it's time to practice. He scoops up his résumé and notebook and heads into an adjacent room. A video camera is rolling so that Eggleston and his coach can review his performance. Across the table, Sherri Gibson of OhioMeansJobs is smiling.

They exchange pleasantries. Eggleston hands her a copy of his new résumé and his portfolio, neatly put together in a plastic three-ring binder. The first few questions are pretty standard.

He is quiet but confident, and quickly seems to win Gibson over.

Then she throws him a curveball: "If you were a tree, any kind of tree, what would you be, and why?"

Without missing a beat, Eggleston answers. "An oak," he says. "Very strong, very sturdy."

"I like that," says Gibson, smiling. When Eggleston mentions he's missed only two days of work in the last six years, she exclaims, "You're hired!"

The interview training is a success.

But of course Eggleston isn't really hired for anything yet. No one in Coshocton County has a clear idea of what jobs workers like Eggleston would even apply for. And that, critics say, is the core problem with relying on retraining programs to address worker dislocation amid the sweeping change in the power sector. Retrain for what, exactly?

LOCATED IN EASTERN OHIO, Coshocton has a mix of rural landscape and industrial labor common to much of Appalachia. It has rolling green hills and the occasional farm stand; it's a place where people take pride in making things. And like so many communities in Appalachia, it's deeply shaped by coal.

The Conesville power plant began burning coal to generate electricity in 1957. Over time, the plant grew to include six coal-fired boilers that could churn out nearly 1,600 megawatts of power. At its peak, the plant employed six hundred workers.

The plant manager, Ryan Forbes, has worked at Conesville for twelve years. Shortly after he took the manager's job, AEP announced it was moving up the timetable for the plant's retirement. He will now oversee its closure.

"I've had four family members make lifelong careers here at Conesville, so it's definitely close to me," he said.

Forbes said the plant would have just ninety-five workers by the summer of 2020. About twenty-five employees had found jobs elsewhere within the AEP system, and some were retiring.

The power plant's three massive smokestacks have been a fixture of the small town's landscape for decades, alongside a convenience store, a post office, and a school. Dalton Summers, the superintendent of the River View Local School District, said having the power plant in the district was a huge advantage.

"When you have a power plant in your district, it's almost a separate tax source," he said.

Until recently, Conesville was valued at $72.2 million, and it paid a significant amount of property tax and a state utility tax to the county and school district. Of River View's $22.1 million annual budget, 10 percent comes from the power plant.

Because of that high level of local funding, Summers said, River View has traditionally received less funding from the state. Still, the millions paid by the plant locally in taxes made that a worthwhile trade-off.

"River View was able to offer a lot of things that a lot of rural communities wouldn't be able to offer," he said, including eight advanced-placement courses at the high school, three foreign languages, a swim team, and small class sizes.

The last time the district built a new school, it didn't have to ask local taxpayers to chip in. In fact, Summers said the district hasn't asked for a new operating levy in more than twenty-five years.

But the looming closure has already started to erode that funding. In October 2017, the Ohio Department of Taxation devalued the plant from $72.2 million to $34.7 million, resulting in a $1 million revenue loss for the school district. When the plant is fully closed, the district is expected to lose $2.2 million.

"We tell people, if you just take ten percent out of your own income, you're going to have to make adjustments to that," Summers said. One adjustment: River View will likely close one of its four elementary schools. In order to avoid other cuts, Summers expects the district will need to ask for additional taxpayer support.

Conesville's closure is more than just a financial blow, he added. AEP has been a partner to the schools. If the schools needed something, he could call.

"It's not going to just affect the school in the sense of money," Summers said. "We have a lot of kids' parents that work for this plant, and this could cause relocation."

Summers said he thinks this closure, unlike some of the others the region has weathered, is different.

"Make no mistake, it is a big impact. Any plant that closes in a small community is a big impact," he said. "A plant like AEP, with the level of jobs that it did provide, the good livings people made that work there, the tax base to the schools—it's really big."

SINCE 2010, more than a dozen coal-fired power plants have closed in Ohio alone. Gilbert Michaud, an assistant professor at the George V. Voinovich School of Leadership and Public Affairs at Ohio University, has studied the associated impacts of these closures.

"These are huge economic drivers in the regions that they're in," he said. Not only do the power stations employ hundreds of workers; they have a ripple effect through the use of vendors and their supply chains.

The Conesville plant was a significant purchaser of Ohio coal, much of it mined by Westmoreland Coal Company. In late 2018, Westmoreland joined the list of mining companies that have declared bankruptcy. "A lot of these rural communities that don't have very diverse economies, these are core industries and core facilities that are really driving economic development and jobs in these regions," Michaud said.

He and colleagues published a study that examined the effects of the closure of two Dayton Power and Light coal-fired power plants in Adams County, in southern Ohio. They found the county and local governments and school districts were set to lose $8.5 million in tax revenues due to the closures. The closure of the plant itself meant the loss of 370 direct jobs, as well as more than 700 associated jobs indirectly supported by the plant.[3]

To gauge those workers' prospects, the researchers constructed what's called a "skill-shed" analysis, looking at the region's occupations that have some sort of competitive edge, and whether those jobs were projected to be in demand. They then compared those to the skill sets of the power plant workers.

"We did find that there were emerging industry clusters in things like tourism and rural health care," Michaud said. "But the problem here is that these folks would face a wage challenge if they were to transition to new careers altogether."

In other words, they could expect to earn a lot less. If they want to find work in their skill sets that pays something close to their old jobs, many of them would likely have to travel. The analysis found that blue-collar workers would have a ninety-five-mile commute, on average, to find comparable work. White-collar workers would need to travel about 175 miles.

"And so a lot of these folks have been moving away, both within Ohio and out of state altogether, unfortunately," Michaud said.

That's accelerating both population loss in small towns and the trend toward greater concentration of jobs in the region's cities.

BOBBY BOWMAN LIVES IN WELCH, West Virginia, where he worked in coal mines for about twelve years before his last employer, the Pinnacle Mine, shut down in 2018. About six hundred jobs were eliminated. Bowman started looking into other local options, which were slim.

Bowman remembers the town of Welch as bustling when he was younger, with businesses lining both sides of the streets. Not anymore.

"You can come and drive down the street in Welch, and there's about four or five businesses now on just the main street, McDowell Street," he said.

Bowman had been with the UMWA for years and opted for a retraining program the union offers to get a certification in heavy-equipment operation.

He speaks highly of the training staff and stays in touch with several people he met in the four-week program at the UMWA Career Center in Prosperity, Pennsylvania.

Clemmy Allen has been retraining coal miners in the UMWA's training centers for more than thirty years. A Department of Labor grant provides $5,000 in tuition assistance and a $20 daily stipend to West Virginia miners who have been laid off or lost their jobs. Allen said thousands of miners have taken advantage of the program, but, he acknowledged, it's also limited. "To go into training and not have money to, you know, meet their monthly obligations," he said, "is very, very difficult.

"We never have enough resources—never," he said.

With his new training and certification, Bowman headed back home to southern West Virginia to look for work. But the few places hiring wanted more experience or required specialized knowledge of certain types of equipment that he didn't yet have.

"It just didn't materialize, and I don't guess that's where I was meant to be," Bowman said.

So he tried retraining again, this time paying his own way through a truck-driving school in nearby Beckley. He found work briefly with a state road construction project, then took a position delivering gasoline to service stations. He likes the work. He has insurance and gets to come home every night. But it doesn't offer the same pay or benefits he had as a miner.

Still, he thinks of himself as lucky. He's watched other former miners move away or struggle to find work. One he knows of is living in a camper at a nearby campground, unable to afford any other housing.

WORK RETRAINING is the go-to response from the region's lawmakers whenever a power plant, mine, or manufacturing business closes, and it figures prominently in political plans for a transition from fossil fuels, like the Green New Deal. But several officials and economists in the Appalachian region have grown wary of how much retraining can achieve. Miners and power plant workers who made salaries ranging from $60,000 to $75,000 a year are now looking at options paying $12 or $15 an hour.

Josh Benton is deputy secretary of Kentucky's Education and Workforce Development Cabinet. He said the state has had some success retraining people to work in the health-care industry, but it's hard to find jobs near where those displaced workers live.

"The challenge that we face is not necessarily, 'Are the training programs effective?'" he said. "It's, 'Are there other industries where those displaced workers can go?'"

None of this comes as a surprise to Gordon Lafer. Lafer, a political economist and associate professor at the University of Oregon's Labor Education and Research Center, has written widely on issues of labor and employment policy.

"The most important thing to know about job-training programs is that they don't create jobs," Lafer said.

In the wake of NAFTA and other free-trade agreements in the 1990s, Lafer wrote *The Job Training Charade* in 2002, which he called the first comprehensive critique of the track record for American job-training policies going back to the early 1960s. He detailed how such programs had failed over and over to ease the pain of economic dislocation brought by globalization, automation, and other forces that cause mass displacement.

"And if there's ever an example of the impotence and uselessness of writing books, that's one of them," he said with a laugh. He calls job training an "undead policy."

"You can drive a stake through its heart and it keeps coming back up. And I think it's because it's so useful politically. Anytime there's some kind of crisis of unemployment or low wages, job training is one of the favorite things of both Democrats and Republicans, because it's cheap, it's symbolic," Lafer said. "But it's never worked as a response to unemployment or low wages."

More than that, Lafer argues, the rhetoric around worker retraining actually makes it harder to address core issues.

"It kind of places the blame on workers instead of employers, because it suggests, 'If only you had the right skills, or the right work ethic, or something, then you wouldn't be in the trouble you're in.'"

Think of Bobby Bowman, the former miner who put in twelve years digging coal and then paid his own way to learn a new trade. Or Joe Eggleston, who barely missed a day of work at the Conesville power plant. What did they do wrong? Nothing, Lafer says. They worked hard, made profits for their companies, and added value to their communities. And while those men are taking their current hard circumstances with grace, they have a right to be angry, says Lafer. The worker-training programs largely serve to defuse that anger.

"This is used to try to get people to be less angry, you know, at a moment when people are losing their jobs. And they're really pissed off," he said. "And the truth is, it would be better for that anger not to be defused but to be focused on a demand for something that is concrete, and that is really going to produce decently paying jobs."

When Lafer casts an eye on current economic statistics, he sees job growth but little growth in wages and erosion of health benefits, pensions, and other forms of worker security.

And when he looks to future trends, he sees a big potential problem ahead.

"I think automation is a serious issue, a serious problem," he said. "And I don't think worker training is the solution."

ANDRE WOODSON threaded his way through the yellow bins in a vast Amazon warehouse filled with boxes and envelopes to be packed, sorted, and shipped. In Amazon-speak, this is a "fulfillment center."

"Our Jeffersonville, Indiana, fulfillment center is about 1.2 million square feet, which is equivalent to about twenty-eight football fields," Woodson explained.

A former college football standout, Woodson was drafted into the NFL and played a few years with the New York Giants and the Washington Redskins. Woodson now applies his discipline to staying on company talking points as an Amazon public relations representative.

About 2,500 people work here, just across the Ohio River from Louisville, Kentucky. But looking out across the floor, it's sometimes hard to find a human among the boxes, bins, and conveyor belts.

The Amazon warehouse, or "fulfillment center," in Jeffersonville, Indiana, is the size of twenty-eight football fields and employs about 2,500 people. Jobs like these are at risk of replacement by automation.

"So here at our ergonomic pack stations, our great associates interact with the technology to package customers' orders," Woodson said as a nearby employee scanned items. A computer shows the optimal box size to be packaged. "The tape machine will push out the perfect amount of tape so they can seal the box," he said.

There are about twenty Amazon fulfillment and distribution centers like this one in the surrounding area. Some are their host town's main employer. Just south of this facility, in Campbellsville, Kentucky, a town of about eleven thousand, around 20 percent of the local workforce is employed at an Amazon warehouse.

The Brookings Institution analyzed employment data and found more than twenty towns around the country where more than 5 percent of the workforce is employed in e-commerce.[4] About 15 percent of workers in Ottawa, Kansas, are employed at distribution centers operated by Walmart and American Eagle. In Mount Vernon, Illinois, warehouses account for almost a tenth of all jobs.

These have been credited with breathing new life into small heartland towns that were bleeding jobs and population, countering the mass migration to large cities. However, these towns are again vulnerable to displacement and unemployment because of automation.

"We have a lot of what we call 'pick and pack' warehouse facilities, and those facilities have a lot of people in them, but they also have a lot of computers and robots," Michael Gritton said. He's executive director at KentuckianaWorks, a nonprofit organization focused on workforce development in Kentucky and Indiana.

"Over time, we expect those facilities to have fewer people and more computers and robots," Gritton continued. He's concerned about what that means for the region, as more people become reliant on jobs with lower wages and irregular schedules. "That doesn't seem to be a recipe for a happy Kentucky," he said, "or a happy America."

And it's not just warehouse jobs at risk. A number of reports about the future of work amid the far broader application of "smart automation" and artificial intelligence have grabbed headlines with their projections about potential job losses.

Mark Muro was lead author of one such report for the Brookings Institution that found a wide range of vulnerable occupations, from truck drivers (self-driving vehicles) to the financial sector (AI and algorithms).

He said the next wave of automation will be different from previous experience with automation in the United States, when relatively simple robotics took over some manufacturing jobs. Cheaper technologies with greater capabilities have the potential to reach into a much wider range of industries.

"Technologies can replace things that we thought might be durable for longer," he said. Food service jobs, hotel jobs, even jobs in HR and business services look vulnerable. "And we're concerned because these are the jobs that are the anchors of our low-income workforce."

Past waves of automation have brought great change to the US labor force but also coincided with overall job growth. Muro said the likeliest scenarios for automation in the coming decades are for a further hollowing out of jobs, rather than wholesale loss, and an unequal distribution of effects. Small towns and rural areas will likely have less capability to adapt because they offer fewer job options and have generally lower education levels.

However, Muro said, technological possibility does not equal reality—and policy really matters.

"These are human devices, these technologies," he said. "We as a society need to decide how we want to use them."

There is, to put it mildly, significant debate about what impact automation will have, or even what impact it has had already. Some argue that globalization and free trade had a greater impact on job losses in manufacturing than did automation—a debate that has flared up among Democratic contenders in the 2020 presidential race.

But whether the cause of displacement is automation and AI, or trade, or the coming transition away from fossil fuels, it seems that we in America simply do not do this transition thing very well, despite all the political rhetoric and government funding. Ask anyone in steel towns from Gary, Indiana, to Braddock, Pennsylvania, or Youngstown, Ohio.

BRICK BUILDINGS LINE the wide sidewalks of Main Street in downtown Coshocton. On a spring day, dogwood trees are blooming and bright red and white tulips dot the grassy public square, home to the local courthouse and a gazebo.

There are barbershops, an optometrist, a florist. A railroad-themed steak house is open for lunch. A trendy public art installment features a small roller coaster designed and built by the local high school and a marquee that blinks "Be nice to others."

But there are also vacant buildings along the main drag, signs of the downturn the town has weathered.

Paula Wagner has lived in Coshocton for more than forty years. She taught Spanish at a local high school for thirty-five years. Standing on

Main Street, she says Coshocton has been a wonderful place to live, but it isn't thriving like it once was.

"We still have some businesses, but every time one of these big businesses goes out, it takes so many people. They have to move to find other jobs outside of town, or they'll move their whole family," she said.

Denise Guthrie owns Mercantile on Main, where she has sold cotton quilting materials for twenty years. Now, with the power plant closing, she's worried.

"It's an integral part of the community," Guthrie said. A Coshocton native, she greets everyone who comes through her doors like she knows them, largely because she does. Many of her customers, or their families, have worked at the power plant.

"We're hurting," she said. "I remember what it was, you know, but that was the past."

Guthrie knows firsthand what that loss looks like. Her husband was laid off when the paper mill closed.

"It's like, bam, bam, bam, you know, our community is hit; you see that," she said.

In recent years, the community has tried to diversify.

"We have a lot to offer," said Guthrie. Local wineries have banded together to create a wine trail, and a brewery has opened. Visitors can visit historic Roscoe Village, a restored nineteenth-century canal town, and hunting and fishing opportunities abound. Coshocton County is home to a Kraft Heinz food processing plant and an American flag producer, Annin Flagmakers, as well as more than a dozen smaller manufacturers.

"I will say, we're resilient, we'll survive, we'll find jobs, somehow we find jobs, we find new opportunities," Guthrie said. "But it is a concern."

County and local officials haven't been sitting idly by as Conesville's closure approaches.

Inside a former hotel now converted to office space, Amy Stockdale, executive director of the Coshocton Chamber of Commerce, sits with Tiffany Swigert, executive director of the Coshocton Port

Authority, and Sherri Gibson, who gave Joe Eggleston his mock job interview.

"This group of ladies sitting right here, we have a really strong united front locally as to how we're going to help our community through any type of loss," Swigert said.

All of these women work with the local business community. They've each been personally affected by a past business closure in the region.

"We have had moments of heartache and then picked ourselves back up and said, 'Okay, we can pull through this, we're going to be able to do it,'" she said. "And we've done it quite well in the past."

As AEP prepares to close the Conesville plant, they have devised a multipronged plan to help the community, one that borrows heavily from their experience dealing with past manufacturing losses. It includes working to identify sites for new manufacturers and cleaning up existing brownfield sites to boost the tax base. Swigert admits the efforts, driven in part by grant funding, are in the early stages.

For workers facing unemployment, OhioMeansJobs and Coshocton County's Department of Job and Family Services have stepped in to offer résumé writing and interviewing classes at the Conesville plant.

"I think it's really important to recognize that these employees, a lot of them graduated high school and went straight to AEP afterward," Swigert said. "It's not that they don't necessarily know how to interview or create a good résumé, but they never had to."

The local branch of Central Ohio Technical College hosts job fairs. Gibson said interest in employing laid-off AEP workers is running high.

"Just with the initial rumors of AEP closing, the surrounding counties lit up on my phone because they know that these workers are loyal, and that they're faithful, and that they're skilled," she said.

Heidi Binko, executive director and cofounder of the Just Transition Fund, a nonprofit that works with coal communities undergoing their transition, said as a growing number of communities find themselves facing coal plant or mine closures, it's smart to throw everything they have at what comes next.

"There is no one silver bullet, right?" she said. "There is not one thing that is going to work."

Gilbert Michaud agrees. Local economic development organizations and others in Ohio are heavily involved in supporting workers affected by coal plant closures, he says. But as his research has shown, Coshocton is facing some long odds.

"A lot of these communities, we found, haven't really fully been able to bounce back to what they once were after a large coal plant closes," he said. Rural communities are smart to offer technical assistance and job training, but it will take more than that.

"Basically, give folks options so they aren't forced to leave," Michaud says. "I think that there's a lot of people who really care about these issues, and that really love these rural Appalachian communities and counties, and that are trying to do things to help enhance the well-being of the folks that live there and keep them in the region."

4.
Pike County, Black Lung, and the Costs of Coal

THE WELCOME SIGN for Pike County informs you that you've entered "America's Energy Capital." Pike County is in the heart of Kentucky's Appalachian coalfields, and it's home to the offices of Dr. James Brandon Crum. A proud son of a coal-mining family, Crum is a radiologist, and much of his job deals with one of the hidden costs of that energy—a cost carried in the lungs of the men and women who dig the coal.

Crum is certified to read the lung X-rays of coal miners who suspect they have black lung disease. This entirely preventable occupational disease had been on the decline in recent years, after decades of progress in reduced dust exposure and increased health monitoring. Or so many medical officials thought.

But in one X-ray after another Crum was seeing something that did not fit that narrative: miners with black lung, often the most advanced and deadly form of the disease, called progressive massive fibrosis.

"So this is what the X-ray of you and I or a normal person should look like," Crum told NPR reporter Howard Berkes as he pulled up a set of healthy-lung images.[1] Then he showed X-ray images of the lungs of a miner he had recently diagnosed, littered with white splotches.

"There are these large conglomerate masses, consistent with complicated black lung."

Over a little less than two years, Crum's small clinic found this worst form of black lung disease in sixty miners.

Crum contacted officials at the National Institute for Occupational Safety and Health, where he was met with some skepticism. After all, as NIOSH epidemiologist Scott Laney would point out, the rate of severe black lung that Crum was describing was "unprecedented by any historical standard."

As the NPR investigation showed, and Laney and other researchers would later confirm, Crum was right. Black lung was roaring back, with cases pouring in from clinics across central Appalachia.

A NIOSH study followed up on Crum's patients and other cases identified in an investigation by NPR and the Ohio Valley ReSource. The researchers found that the rate of black lung disease among experienced miners in central Appalachia is now the highest it has been in a quarter century, with cases concentrated among miners in Kentucky, Virginia, and West Virginia.[2]

Nationally, the rate of black lung among miners is about one in ten. "In central Appalachia, it's about one in five, which is really concerning," said epidemiologist Cara Halldin, who supervises the coal workers' health surveillance program for NIOSH and was one of the study authors.

By the spring of 2017, Laney and other NIOSH researchers had returned to Pike County, this time to spread the word about the sharp increase in a disease that should have been on its way to the history books.[3]

"If we come to your town, there's generally something bad going on there," Laney said as he prepared to address an auditorium of medical students at the University of Pikeville. Pike County, America's Energy Capital, is "at the epicenter of one of the largest industrial medicine disasters that the United States has ever seen," Laney told them.

THE X-RAY THAT CRUM had shared in his clinic was from an eastern Kentucky miner named Mackie Branham Jr.[4] Branham's story is in some ways typical of miners who end up with the disease. He entered the mines straight out of high school.

"Turned down a full scholarship to go to college, because I knowed I'd go straight in and make good money," Branham said. "I wanted to start my own family."

Branham and his wife, Amber, have five affectionate children. When it came time for a picture, four of the boys piled onto an overstuffed sofa with Mackie and Amber. A self-described "company man," Branham did whatever the company asked, and that often meant extremely long hours. He missed birthdays and holidays to pick up extra shifts. He said he'd sometimes work more than twenty-four hours straight.

Kentucky coal miner Mackie Branham Jr. and his wife, Amber Branham, in the home where they're raising five children. At thirty-eight years old, Branham was diagnosed with the advanced form of black lung disease.

Like many miners with the complicated form of the disease, Branham can't make it through a full sentence before sucking in a short breath. Talking makes him feel like he's "trying to blow up a new balloon." But unlike most afflicted miners, who are typically in their fifties or sixties before symptoms reach this stage, Branham was just thirty-eight years old.

"I can no longer provide for my family," he said. "I can't get out and do nothing around the house like I normally would with them. It tears your nerves up."

Branham applied for black lung benefits, but his former employer, Alpha Natural Resources, was fighting to deny his claim.

"A lot of people don't know what it's like to have your babies sittin' there and you can't even hardly put food on the table," he said.

Amber Branham had taken a waitressing job at the Gold Ring Diner in Elkhorn City to help pay bills. "I make in a week what he made in two days," she said. "It's just a hard thing to watch, because I've seen a strong man going from working five, six, seven days a week—all the hours they want—down to havin' to be home twenty-four seven 'cause he can't stand the weather outside."

Mackie Branham listens and then looks up.

"I can't provide for nobody no more." He draws a shallow breath, then continues. "That takes my manhood away."

"It doesn't take your manhood away," Amber replied. "This family, as you can see, the kids respect every bit of him."

"It takes my pride away, all right?"

Amber said he's not the only coal miner that feels that way.

"There's hundreds of men out there that think that 'Oh, I can't provide, so I'm worthless.' They're not worthless because their families love them and want them to be here as long as they can have them here," she said. "But in their eyes, they get depressed because they can't do what they've always done."

US COAL MINERS have long had to fight for protection from and treatment for black lung. In Great Britain, the government compensated miners for coal-related lung disease as early as the 1940s. But in the United States, miners faced resistance not just from the industry but from the medical community, which cast doubt on workers' claims and the legitimacy of the disease itself, which was often dismissed or blamed on other factors, such as smoking.[5]

That began to change in the late 1960s, after the Farmington mine disaster in West Virginia, an explosion that killed seventy-eight workers. The disaster galvanized advocates and miners who pressed for a range of mine safety improvements, including measures to address black lung. Unhappy with the state and federal government response, and even that of their own union, miners worked with sympathetic physicians to form black lung associations.

These associations lobbied the West Virginia legislature for a fund to compensate sick miners. But it took a statewide strike by some forty thousand West Virginia miners in 1969 before the state legislature passed the first bill to care for miners made sick from coal dust exposure. Later that year, Congress followed up with the Coal Mine Health and Safety Act, which limited dust exposure and created a benefits system for sick miners and their widows.

It took a while to see results, given the latency period between exposure and onset of the disease, but eventually black lung rates began to drop.

"You know, I thought this was going to be a disease that you read about only in the history books," said Dr. Edward Petsonk, a professor at West Virginia University and a pulmonologist who also worked with NIOSH. "This disease was supposed to have been eradicated."

But in 2003 Petsonk noticed an uptick in cases. After decades of steady progress, the miners in central Appalachia were showing more signs of the disease. By 2010 Petsonk and other researchers had determined that the prevalence of black lung disease had roughly doubled.

The disastrous explosion at Massey Energy's Upper Big Branch Mine in West Virginia in 2010 gave gruesome testimony to that. Autopsies of the twenty-nine men killed in the explosion revealed that some

71 percent of those killed already had signs of the disease in their lungs, some of them as young as their thirties.[6]

Gary Wayne Quarles of Naoma, West Virginia, was one of them. His father, Gary Quarles, also a miner, said his son had been in the mines for thirteen years before the explosion that ended his life.

"He worked when he first came out of high school at a sawmill, just for a little while. And then he went to work underground," Quarles said. He was still grieving his son's loss when he got news about the autopsy results. "He already had black lung."

From 2016 to 2018, the Ohio Valley ReSource team joined NPR investigative reporter Berkes in his effort to learn more about the extent of the black lung resurgence and what had caused it. By combing through records supplied directly by Appalachian health and legal clinics, Berkes found more than 2,300 cases of the severe form of black lung disease, more than twenty times the amount reported by the federal agency in charge of monitoring the disease.[7]

Berkes and the ReSource team interviewed dozens of affected miners about their working conditions and what living with the disease really meant.

Virginia miner Jackie Yates said his father and older brother were also miners. His brother died from the disease he now has. "It's hard to breathe," he said. "I'll go to coughing real bad, coughing to the point of almost throwing up."

Yates is a lean man with a penetrating gaze and the direct manner of someone who has dealt with his share of hardships. At age forty-nine, Yates was diagnosed with the complicated, or severe, form of black lung disease.

"But I made my choice when I was nineteen years old to work in the coal mines," Yates said. "And if cancer don't take me, or a wreck on a street won't take me, coal mines will."

The work, he said, was always dusty, and not just the black dust from coal. He described white dust from the surrounding layers of rock piling up like ashes on his helmet and clogging his protective mask. The rock dust increased as the remaining coal seams grew thinner.

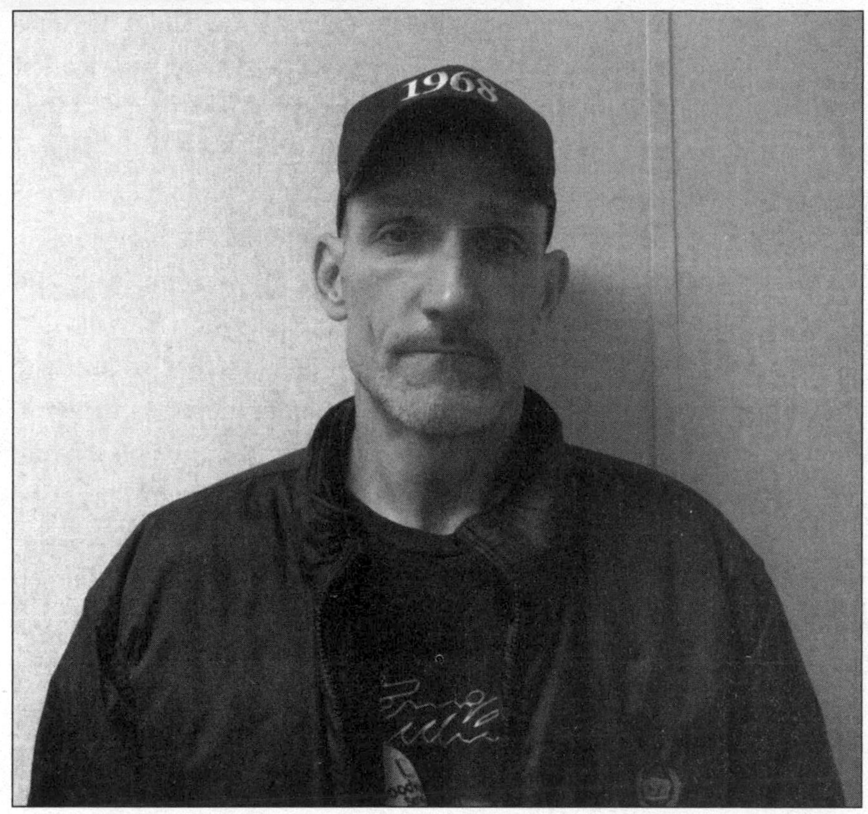

After twenty years of working underground, coal miner Jackie Yates learned that he has the severe form of black lung disease. "I made my choice when I was nineteen years old to work in the coal mines," Yates said. "And if cancer don't take me, or a wreck on a street won't take me, coal mines will."

"Nowadays, all the good coal—we call it the 'gravy coal,' that the companies like to see 'cause you cut it fast and it don't create a lot of dust—all that's gone," Yates said. "It's a little seam here, a little seam there, and a lot of rock in the middle. That's just all that's left."

That rock dust, containing silica, or quartz, is generated when powerful mining equipment tears through the layers of rock near the coal. It is far more toxic than coal dust alone, say researchers—up to twenty times more so.

During the Obama administration, the federal government strengthened the regulation of coal dust exposure in a major victory for worker health after years of industry obstruction and delay.[8] But the rule failed to directly control exposure to silica dust. Berkes found that, despite decades of warnings about the toxicity of silica dust, and even evidence of clusters of disease linked to silica exposure, neither the coal industry nor the federal agency charged with regulating it, the Mine Safety and Health Administration, took action.

Miner after miner we interviewed also talked about widespread cheating by coal companies when it came to requirements to monitor dust in the mines. Some said conditions would be good on the rare dates when the company knew a state or federal inspector might be on-site. But the rest of the time, they ate dust. Others described seeing dust-monitoring devices placed in sheltered spots, such as in lunch pails or separate rooms, so as to indicate cleaner air on the reports turned in to government regulators.

That was the sort of activity federal prosecutors alleged at a Kentucky mine in 2018. Eight employees of the now-bankrupt Armstrong Energy coal company were indicted on charges that they falsified dust-monitoring samples after a whistleblower alerted federal regulators of tampering.[9]

In 2018, the National Academy of Sciences issued a report saying that the coal mining industry needs a "fundamental shift" in the way it controls exposure to coal and silica dust in order to prevent lung disease among miners.[10]

Lee Petsonk, who had recognized the rise in disease fifteen years earlier, agrees.

"It's just not acceptable to have this level of disease and death in an industry and not see a really serious response," he said. "This is just not what we as a society have promised our working people."

JERRY HELTON, age sixty-five, has short-cropped gray hair and is quick to show a smile. The former coal miner is remarkably upbeat given what he has recently gone through. The first symptoms came on suddenly.

"Labor Day weekend of 2010, that's when I noticed my breathing was just a little bit different. Then about a couple weeks later, I got to where I couldn't hardly breathe," he said. "The doctors say my lungs started shutting down, they said they were hardened just like a lump of coal."[11]

Helton would undergo a double lung transplant, a risky and costly surgery.

"I went into a coma," Helton recalled. "They kept me on machines for three weeks."

He lost muscle function and couldn't even lift his head. His kidneys shut down, and he now relies on dialysis treatments and is seeking a donor for a kidney transplant. It's an ongoing process to regain control of his body, but Helton is now up and walking. And, most important, he now has lungs that work.

"My breathing is wonderful," he said. "It's great. I can breathe."

He has a farm where he's been keeping sheep, and he's looking to expand and get into raising cattle. His therapy is helping him walk more normally, and he's even back in his preferred footwear.

"When I left the hospital, I couldn't get my boots on. I wore tennis shoes and hated them," he said. "I'm a boot man!"

Helton's boots gently thud as he walks down the hall, the sound of a minor miracle. But it came at a steep price.

"The doctors, they sort of laugh and joke and said they wanted to check me out and see if I was worthy of spending millions on," he said.

In 2018, NIOSH researchers Laney and Halldin and their colleague David Blackley published a study on the dramatic increase in lung transplant surgeries for miners with black lung.[12] This is what they found: sixty-two miners with black lung disease had lung transplant surgery over the past two decades; most of them lived in Kentucky, Virginia, and West Virginia.

"In the last decade the rate of lung transplants for patients with black lung increased nearly threefold," Blackley said. "That suggested pretty strongly to us that this is a problem that's getting worse."

More than two dozen patients were placed on a wait list for transplants. Of those, eleven died while waiting.

The study also looked into who paid for lung transplants. Insurance from coal companies and other private sources covered about a third of the transplant costs. Almost two-thirds were paid for with public insurance, including 26 percent paid for by Medicare and up to 24 percent paid for by the federal Black Lung Disability Trust Fund.

That fund has paid more than $45 billion over the last fifty-plus years to cover benefits for miners who can't seek benefits from their employers because the responsible companies have either gone bankrupt or can't be identified. The fund paid $184 million in 2017 alone. It's a lifeline for more than twenty-five thousand miners and their widows and dependents.

And the fund is in trouble.

A 2018 report from the Government Accountability Office found that the trust fund could go $15 billion in debt over the next thirty years after the reduction of a tax on the coal industry that supported the fund.[13]

The trust fund is mainly supported by a tax on each ton of coal mined, but the tax has not covered costs, frequently leaving the fund with deficits of billions. In 2008 Congress absorbed about $6.5 billion of the fund's debt into the general budget, meaning taxpayers bailed out the fund.

In 1981, Congress approved a temporary tax increase on coal in hopes of getting the trust fund out of debt. As the debts persisted, the increase was extended. It was set to expire again at the end of 2018, cutting the fund's income by more than half just as the scope of the resurgence of black lung disease was coming into full view.

That set up a test for Kentucky's powerful senior senator, Mitch McConnell.

As Senate majority leader, McConnell could find a way to extend the tax rate. During an October 2018 event in eastern Kentucky he appeared to indicate he would do that.[14]

"That'll be taken care of before we get into an expiration situation," McConnell said in response to a ReSource reporter's question. "It just won't be allowed to be unfunded," McConnell reiterated.

But as time passed with no action, miners' health advocates grew nervous. In a written statement to the ReSource, McConnell said, "It is a top priority of mine to maintain and protect benefits for those suffering from black lung disease."

On a cool but clear November day in 2018, about a dozen residents from eastern Kentucky's coal mining region crowded into the small entranceway of an office building in the town of London, Kentucky, where McConnell has his local field office.

McConnell's staff let the local advocates for black lung treatment into the office a few at a time to make their case for full funding for the black lung trust fund.

Morgan Brown said she was visiting McConnell's office on behalf of her father, a retired coal miner suffering from black lung. Brown said her father worked for different coal companies across the state. Now he struggles with the disease and fights to get benefits from the industry.

"You thought these were your employers, they cared about you," she said. "Just to see them fight so hard against him is just, like I said, it's infuriating. You just really feel anger."

Retired miner Carl Shoupe said that if anyone can get Congress to act, it's his state's senior senator.

"Senator McConnell, he's the most powerful senator in the world, as far as that goes. And if he gets on this, he can push it through. I believe that," Shoupe said.

But McConnell was in an uncomfortable position that pit the interests of powerful home-state mining companies against those sickened by work in that industry.

The industry had been arguing behind the scenes in Washington and in regional opinion pages that the coal tax at its current rate was "an unfair burden" and should be allowed to expire.[15]

Tyler White, president of the Kentucky Coal Association, said that would not mean the tax is going away; rather, it would go back to the level Congress originally intended.

"Extending current higher tax rates beyond their scheduled expiration—we kind of look at that as a tax increase at a time when we're still experiencing a significant economic stress," White said.

McConnell has reason to listen when the coal industry speaks. Coal mining companies and their political action committees doled out more than $20 million in political spending in the last two election cycles, according to an analysis of campaign finance records by the nonprofit Center for Responsive Politics. About 95 percent of campaign contributions went to Republicans, and some of the top contributing companies have a major presence in Kentucky, including Alliance Resource Partners and Murray Energy.

Alliance is the third-largest coal producer in the eastern United States, and its CEO, Joe Craft, has groomed close relationships with Republican leaders. Craft's wife, Kelly Craft, is the Trump administration's ambassador to the United Nations. Scott Pruitt, former head of the EPA under Trump, was Craft's guest in courtside seats at a University of Kentucky basketball game.

Bob Murray, CEO of Murray Energy, donated $300,000 to Trump's inauguration and wrote a memo to the White House that he called an "action plan" for the industry, with more than a dozen recommended rollbacks to environmental and worker safety regulations.[16] Those included a request to revise "the arbitrary coal mine dust rule," which Murray said "threatens the destruction of thousands of coal mining jobs."

The mining industry's aggressive lobbying appeared to be paying off. A draft version of a House tax bill included a modest one-year extension of the current excise tax rate on coal to support the black lung trust fund.

Then in late November the National Mining Association, the chief lobbying organization for coal companies, sent members of Congress a letter urging them to remove that section from the bill. The letter from NMA president Hal Quinn warned that if the provision was not removed, NMA "will include this floor vote in its Congressional Scorecard" as a negative mark against lawmakers.[17]

When House Republicans released a new version of the bill a few weeks later, the coal tax rate extension was gone. McConnell did not raise the matter in the Senate, and at the end of the year, the industry got its wish. The tax rate dropped 55 percent, and the black lung trust fund was on a course for billions in additional debt.

The UMWA argued that allowing the coal tax rate to expire would shift the burden for black lung benefits from the industry to the public and that there was "no reason why we would put the taxpayers on the hook instead."

AS THE MINING INDUSTRY worked to shift the burden of black lung care and compensation onto taxpayers, the full costs of the epidemic rippled out through coal mining communities, landing hardest on the families of sick miners.

When Vickie and Gene Salyers moved into their brand-new trailer, Gene bought Vickie a Crock-Pot and a new broom. "I guess 'cause we had a new house, he thought I needed a new sweeper to go with it," Vickie said.[18]

That was in 2002, when the two were young and in love. By Christmas of 2018, Vickie lived in the trailer alone. The trailer's white facade had grayed after years of exposure to the elements, but she kept the yard neat and there were seasonal decorations up. Inside, her husband's plump armchair sat empty in a corner like a shrine, marking the place where Gene had died.

Gene had black lung disease, earned from years of loading coal onto dusty barges on the Big Sandy River.

For him, the disease manifested slowly. A bit winded on the stairs, maybe, then having to stop to catch his breath on the way to the mailbox. Gene was treated for repeated bouts of bronchitis for years, Vickie said, before anyone suspected black lung might be to blame. On Christmas Eve 2009, Vickie got a call from Gene's doctor. Yes, it was urgent. Yes, they'd have to come to the hospital. It was lung cancer.

Gene cycled through one surgery after another, and the family lost both sources of income as Vickie dropped everything to care for him. When their young son, Zach, could sit with Gene, Vickie would try to arrange some work, cutting someone's lawn or cleaning someone's house, to bring in a few dollars. In one complication from surgery, doctors left Gene with an open wound in his side, which Vickie had to drain and clean and bandage several times a day.

She moved Gene's hospital bed to the corner of the living room so he could watch TV. That's where he died in 2013, in the trailer he and Vickie loved so much.

The federal and state black lung benefits systems exist to support miners like Gene and their dependents. But like many people who suffer from black lung, Gene didn't file for his federal black lung benefits until he was already quite sick. In fact, he was *so* sick that he couldn't travel to the exam that would have allowed him to meet the legal requirements for benefits. That would go on to haunt the Salyers family for years.

Vickie said continuing with the black lung claim seemed just impossible in the overwhelming days and weeks following Gene's death. "They ask you all these questions, and, hello, I'm country! I don't know all this stuff."

But Zach reminded Vickie that filing the paperwork was free, and she could use the benefits money.

Salyers's first claim was denied because Gene had been too sick to get tested, and the judge hadn't known how to handle that wrinkle in the usual procedure. Vickie brought the claim before an administrative law judge, who found in her favor.

But KenWest Terminals, Gene's employer, appealed, arguing that

Gene's lung disease could be attributed to his smoking, not his years of breathing coal dust. The case reached the US Sixth Circuit Court of Appeals.

As Vickie Salyers remembered it, each development in the case brought new anxieties. "They [KenWest Terminals] have so many days to appeal it, and here's what they do: they wait till that last day. You know, you get excited a little bit, and then they wait till that last day and they appeal it. And that starts the process over again. And that went on for two years, I betcha, or longer."

Her lawyer, Evan Smith, who is currently at AppalReD Legal Aid, said the Salyers case was in some ways unique and in others deeply typical. Gene met the medical definition for coal workers' pneumoconiosis (the medical term for black lung disease), but, Smith said, "there can be a tension between what the doctors think the medical consensus is and how the law has defined the conditions that are compensable."

With Smith's help, Salyers started to receive $660 per month, a sum that fails to cover her basic needs. Each month she had to choose between making her trailer payment or paying her utility bills. She was behind on her trailer payments and facing eviction.

"I'm about to lose the only thing that me and my husband had together," Salyers said. "If they had to sit here and see him die, they would not put people through that. They would not. They would just give them the benefits and say it was deserved."

Five years after her husband's death, a court awarded Salyers a total of $83,000, some from her husband's black lung case and some from the widow's case she filed after his death. Vickie held her breath through the 2018 holiday season, and the following spring she finally received $62,000 from her husband's employer. It was more money than she had ever seen. She doesn't know where the other $21,000 is or when she can expect it.

"The black lung benefits process is really adversarial," Smith said. "For people who just kind of file a claim and think they can figure out the system on their own, sadly, they're really at a disadvantage."

THE COAL MINERS gather in the predawn stillness at the First Baptist Church in Whitesburg, Kentucky. Nobody's had enough coffee; there's some discussion about whether there's time to run to McDonald's for a breakfast sandwich before the bus gets there.

The miners are traveling eight hours to Washington, DC, to make their case once more to their representatives in Congress. More than six months after Congress reduced the tax supporting the black lung trust fund, the men and women of coal country are making one final attempt to save the fund from plunging into deep debt. Many of them know the disease will likely kill them, but they want to make sure they, and the next generation of miners, are at least cared for as they die, and that their families will be supported.

Retired miner Shirley Smith is raring to go. The stocky, middle-aged blonde shifts her weight back and forth, scanning the groups of men scattered across the parking lot. You can see the flinty strength she had to develop as one of the first women to work in the coal mines decades ago. Shirley doesn't have black lung disease—at least, she doesn't think she does. She's scared to get tested. But her brother and her dad have it, so she's making the trip for them.

For Danny Fouts, the disease is a constant presence, manifesting as a shortness of breath and a weakness that keeps him from tasks he once found easy. He stays in his parked truck, watching the gathering crowd in his side-view mirror. Beside him, his wife, Jeannie, watches from hers. The two are aloof at first, but over the three-day trip, they open up a bit. Jeannie works as a school bus driver. A lot of her life now involves holding the house and the family and the finances together, as Danny is less and less able to contribute. For his part, Danny is depressed. He's already been knocked down, and he knows it only gets worse from here.

Finally, the coach arrives, helmed by an enthusiastic driver named Ric. The miners pile on. George and Bennie Massie, brothers who are passionate union men and champions of the eastern Kentucky African-

American community, stake out the front seats. Behind them sit two young organizers with the Appalachian Citizens' Law Center, Eric Dixon and Rebecca Shelton, who helped arrange the trip. Then there's Jimmy Moore, the bright-eyed president of the Letcher County Black Lung Association, riding with his wife and daughter. There are widows whose husbands died of the disease; wives tagging along to help their ailing husbands; community members who have volunteered to make the trip just to push miners' wheelchairs around Capitol Hill.

Mostly, spirits are high. One miner, Greg Kelly, gazes out the window, eyes moist. He's sitting by himself, the backpack containing his oxygen tank on the aisle seat, a bulwark between him and the rest of the world. Greg is really sick. Not long ago, he was a strapping guy accustomed to physical labor. Now he says he can scarcely hold his fifteen-pound baby grandson. Greg has gone to DC before, and he knows this trip will likely be his last.

Their first meeting is with Representative John Yarmuth, from Louisville. It takes longer to navigate the halls of Congress than the organizers had bargained for, what with bulky wheelchairs that can take the elevators only one at a time and walking miners who need frequent stops for breath. Finally, dozens of advocates crowd into Yarmuth's sitting room.

The miners tell him about the tax rate on coal companies they want to see reinstated for the black lung fund. Yarmuth is sympathetic. He listens to their stories and even suggests some legislation to expand the types of work that would be protected under current health and safety laws.

But the miners aren't stupid: they know that Kentucky's only Democratic representative has little hope of implementing legislation that would cost the coal industry money. The person they really need to win over is several buildings over, and he's expecting them.

Senator McConnell takes some selfies with the first few groups of miners as they get off the elevators with their wheelchair pushers. He speaks to them for about two minutes. And then he leaves.

Afterward, Kentucky miner Barry Johnson shakes his head in disappointment. "We did get some assurances that benefits wouldn't be cut, but it's kind of hard to put a lot of faith in the statement that everything is going to be okay," Johnson said. McConnell's staffers were polite and engaged, he said. But it stung that the senator himself had only stayed a couple of minutes.

There were more meetings to go to, more elevators to ride, more long walks between buildings. But the main event was over. The miners had made their case to their senator, one of the most powerful elected officials in the country, and had received promises they perceived to be empty.

The bus ride home was less energetic. But as Ric steered the coach around east Kentucky's curving roads, organizer Eric Dixon called the miners to attention. A bill had been introduced in the House by Representatives Bobby Scott of Virginia and Alma Adams of North Carolina, both Democrats. It would restore the 2018 rate for the tax that supports the federal Black Lung Disability Trust Fund. The bill would likely face opposition in the Senate if it passed the House, but in that moment it felt like a victory.

In his window seat, blocked off by his oxygen tank, Greg Kelly smiled.

In late 2019, with McConnell facing a competitive 2020 election, the miners won a brief respite: Congress restored the tax to its full rate, but for just one year. Miners and their allies will again face industry lobbyists when the next spending bill is up for passage.

BACK IN HIS OFFICE in Pikeville, radiologist Brandon Crum—who alerted officials to the alarming rise in black lung—continued with the grim tally of new cases. At a conference of black lung clinicians and regulators he said the previous year had been the worst of his career, as more and more X-rays showed yet more black-and-white evidence of diseased lungs.[19]

"I started out with sixty," he told the conference audience in June

2019. "As of last week, I had two hundred and forty-six cases of complicated black lung in my clinic alone."

But due to a change in the state law made by Kentucky legislators, Crum might not be seeing as many of those X-rays. The new law prohibits him from reading X-rays for some miners seeking state benefits.[20]

Lawmakers changed the process miners must use to qualify for black lung benefits. Mine safety advocates said that will shift the balance in favor of coal companies and could make it harder for those with black lung to get benefits.

Republican state senator Phillip Wheeler is an attorney in Pikeville who represents clients seeking state black lung benefits. "On its face the amendments in relation to black lung law may seem very benign," Wheeler said. "But they have a very nefarious purpose."

Radiologists like Crum are generally considered to be the most qualified to interpret miners' X-rays. Yet the Kentucky legislation bars radiologists from providing diagnoses for state benefits claims. Instead, the legislation requires that X-ray readers also be certified pulmonologists.

When NPR and Ohio Valley ReSource reviewed a list of pulmonologists who qualified under the new law, we found that several had previously testified in contested black lung cases on behalf of coal companies seeking to deny miners' claims.

"I do believe the coal industry is writing this bill to exclude certain doctors that they don't like," Wheeler explained.

Brandon Crum said the new law caught him by surprise. "Throughout the United States I know of nowhere where radiologists are taken completely out of the evaluation for potential black lung disease," he said. "That's what we're primarily trained in."

The bill's language on changes to the black lung benefits system was brought forward by Republican Adam Koenig, who represents a district in northern Kentucky. He told NPR that while writing the bill he "relied on the expertise of those who understand the issue—the industry, coal companies, and attorneys."[21]

Among the groups lobbying for the bill that included those changes was the Kentucky Chamber of Commerce. Joe Craft, CEO of Alliance Resources, was chairman of the chamber.

The American College of Radiologists, a professional organization, asked Kentucky to repeal that portion of the law.[22] "This is a matter of life and death," wrote William T. Thorwarth Jr., a radiologist who serves as the organization's CEO. "We hope that the Kentucky legislature will rescind this new law and work with the medical provider community to save more lives."

Efforts to repeal the new law failed in 2019. In early 2020, the ReSource team reviewed state records on the claims miners filed for black-lung benefits in Kentucky before and after the law took effect. Since that change, the number of Kentucky miners diagnosed by state-approved experts as having the disease fell from 54 percent before the change in the law to just 26 percent after. The ReSource team found that in 2019, 161 benefits claims were filed, but only sixteen coal miners were awarded black-lung benefits. That's the lowest ratio of claims awarded to claims dismissed in the past seven years.[23]

ON A BRIGHT October day with the leaves just beginning to turn, a group of miners and mining families gathered at the riverside park in Whitesburg, Kentucky.

They were there to dedicate a large, gleaming black granite memorial for the local miners who had died of black lung. Some two hundred names are engraved on the stone.[24]

Appalachia has many memorials to miners lost in explosions, cave-ins, and other disasters. People from the region can readily list many from painful memory: Sago, Upper Big Branch, Farmington—disasters that together claimed hundreds of lives, made headlines and history.

Black lung takes thousands of lives, but slowly, and alone, and often without notice. Those miners die in hospitals or rest homes. They die while awaiting the surgery that might have bought a few more years. They die in a bed in the corner of a trailer's living room.

A black lung memorial in Whitesburg, Kentucky, for the local miners. Miner William McCool, who has the disease, proposed the idea for a memorial listing the names of miners who died from black lung—a list he expects to someday join. "It would be a blessing to be with them boys," he said.

After his father died of black lung, William McCool suggested a memorial for those miners, too.

"You know, let's give these men the honor they deserve. Let's not forget them," he said.

McCool is sixty-five and a former coal miner himself. "I've seen a lot of coal go down the beltline," McCool said, pausing to catch his breath between phrases. "Somebody's made money, but the cheapest thing the company's got is the worker. Everything else costs them all kinds of money, but they can get workers."

McCool also suffers from black lung. He expects his name will be on the stone memorial one day, too. "It would be a blessing to be with them boys," he says.

PROFILE:

Marcy Tate's New Beginnings

THE NEW BEGINNINGS Pulmonary Rehabilitation clinic in Norton, Virginia, is very much like any other medical center, except it smells faintly of pineapple turnovers. That's because one of the nurses brought them in to share. It's also set up for a group exercise class.

Occupying every inch of wall space surrounding the hand bikes and treadmills are tidy rows of framed photos, each one of a smiling coal miner in a helmet. What with the smell of homemade pastries and the dozens of beaming portraits, the little room doesn't feel so much like a medical clinic as a group hug.

One by one, eight men shuffle into the room. They're mostly older and very sick. Each one has black lung disease. Some tote oxygen tanks behind them like carry-on bags; some tuck smaller, portable oxygen cartridges under their arms like purses. As each man enters, he's met with an effusive hug and some affectionate quips from the clinic's nurses, and each man's weathered face crinkles and blushes as though he were a schoolboy with a crush.

"These girls are my angels, they really are," one patient says, and you can tell he means it.

Marcy Tate runs this clinic and a handful of others in Kentucky, Virginia, and West Virginia, the hotspots of a surging black lung epidemic. Medical providers have struggled to keep up with demand for rehabilitation services as incidences of disease soar. Since she started New Beginnings in 2013, Marcy has dealt with waiting lists so long that she's just kept opening new clinics to meet the demand.[1]

She's also taken to keeping her car stocked with extra exercise clothes, everyday wear, and outfits fit for schmoozing with politicians, because she's always dashing between one engagement and the next and can never be sure when she might get home. She's just on the cusp of fifty, her lipstick is always perfect, her black hair is never mussed, and when she's talking to you, you feel her total presence like a warm embrace.

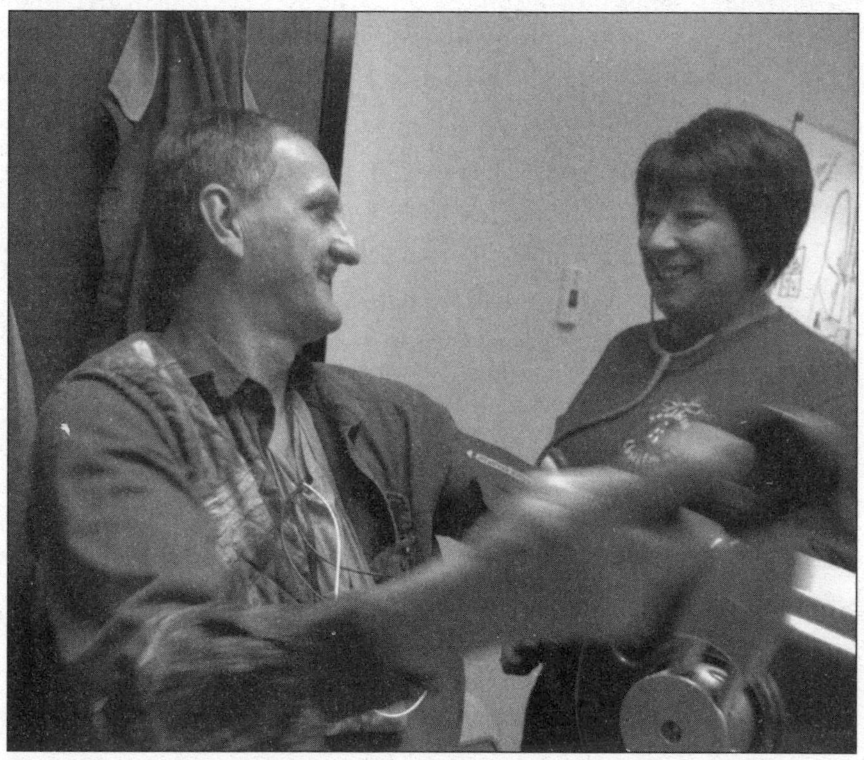

Marcy Tate checks a client's blood pressure during a therapy session at New Beginnings clinic in Norton, Virginia.

"Our guys come together in groups of eight, just like they did in the coal mine," Marcy says. "They're a team again. They get really bonded."

Marcy's brand of pulmonary rehabilitation involves a combination of upper- and lower-body strength exercises, breathing exercises, nutrition education, smoking cessation, and general tips on how to live your life with chronic lung disease.

Her team leads the group through modified exercises on the treadmills and stationary bicycles. It's difficult work for the men, whose lung tissue has been scarred and hardened by the particulates lodged in their bodies.

Just a few minutes into the cardio portion of the class, a man in his fifties clutches the arms of his treadmill, his chest heaving, even though the machine's belt is moving quite slowly. His eyes are wide with panic. Marcy notices. She comes to stand beside him and places a warm hand on his shoulder. She guides him to a seat on the windowsill beside the machine. The man huffs there, eyes downcast, shaking his head.

"He's been out of class for a few sessions," Tate explains. "You really have to keep up with it or you lose your progress."

Marcy is the first to admit her regimen is far from a cure. The way she explains it, pulmonary rehab strengthens healthy lung tissue so the body is more able to compensate for the hardened, scarred tissue impacted by the disease.

Black lung has no cure. When miners begin to show shortness of breath, they might be prescribed an inhaler, and when even that leaves them light-headed, they might progress to a portable oxygen tank. But neither solution is enough. Their scarred lungs can't expand to suck in air, and what air they do manage to inhale can't seep through their lung tissue to nourish their blood. Miners say it's like breathing through a straw or drowning, very slowly, on land.

Roy Ratliff, seventy-two, makes the two-hundred-mile round-trip drive four times a week to attend sessions at New Beginnings. "The breathing's always bad, but it makes me stronger," Ratliff said.

Pulmonary rehab is the only treatment available to Ratliff because he's ineligible for a lung transplant. The risky and expensive procedure is a last-ditch effort to keep miners alive, but even it extends life just three to five years, according to epidemiologists at the National Institute for Occupational Safety and Health.

Worley Clyde Hill, eighty-one, was the second patient to sign up for New Beginnings. Before the program, repeated bouts of pneumonia left him hospitalized for days or weeks at a time.

"Since I came here, I haven't had pneumonia," he says. "I've had a little bit of a sniffle, but nothing bad. It's helped my breathing. And it's helped my stamina; I don't give out as quickly as I did before." Like many miners in advanced stages of black lung, Worley speaks in staccato clauses, punctuated by long pauses as he struggles to inhale. Marcy says one way she tests how far along miners are with the disease is by asking them to say "Mary had a little lamb." If they can get through the sentence in one breath, they're doing okay, all things considered.

After ten minutes or so, the miners climb off their machines and sit in a circle in the center of the room. A nurse leads them through arm-strength routines with light dumbbells. Janie Fortner sits outside in the hallway, a quiet woman of sixty-one whose husband, Jack, suffers from the disease.

The best part of New Beginnings, Janie says, is that Jack feels less isolated and less depressed. "He's not hateful and grouchy like he was, and that makes a better marriage."

5.

Martin County Can't Get Clean Water

MARTIN COUNTY, ON the state line where eastern Kentucky meets West Virginia, should be very rich. Over the past century the county produced more than 436 million tons of coal. That's enough to power 80 million modern homes for a year.[1]

You might think that, sitting on top of that much value, the 11,300 or so people who live in Martin County wouldn't have to worry about getting a clean drink of water.

And yet.

There stood Joe Hammond of the county's water district, once again, in front of an irate crowd, trying to explain why their water was so frequently shut off, discolored, or foul smelling. Why they were so often told to boil water before using it. Why their bills sometimes came with a warning about possible health risks from drinking the water.

Hammond, a mild man with a graying mustache and glasses, tried to explain the county's system for calling customers affected by a cutoff or boil-water advisory. But he was interrupted by an angry man who said people don't get warnings before water is shut off. "I'm done with it—it was a lie!" the man shouted and stormed out.

In Martin County, Kentucky, residents rely on a water treatment plant that was built in 1968 and has been poorly maintained. Frequently, the system would lose more water to leaks than it would deliver to customers, leading to a crisis state regulators called "grim and desperate."

Hammond hadn't even made it to the part about how people in Martin County, one of the country's poorest places, would probably soon have to pay even more for their unreliable water.

On any given day, the water system here was losing more to leaks than it delivered to customers—sometimes up to 70 percent of the total supply. State records showed 113 boil-water notices over a little more than ten years, as well as forty-eight water system violations. At the time of the heated meeting Hammond faced in 2016, the water system was again under scrutiny by the state's public service commission, the third such investigation.[2]

Opening a tap is an exercise in trust, one most of us don't give much thought. We take for granted that the water from our faucets will be safe to use and there when we need it. But in Martin County, many people don't trust a government that can't deliver this most basic service.

"Here's the thing," Gary Ball said. "In 1964, LBJ kicked off the war on poverty." Ball is editor of Martin County's weekly newspaper, the *Mountain Citizen*. President Johnson's visit to Martin County is the stuff of local lore, he said. It not only launched one of his Great Society programs, it shaped the national image of Appalachia, as Johnson sat and talked with local man Tom Fletcher on a run-down cabin porch. That cabin is still here. The poverty Johnson declared war on is still around, too. Nearly 40 percent of the county's residents live in poverty, and per capita income hovers around $15,500 a year. Only about a third of working-age people are employed.[3]

"Here we are, over fifty years later, and we can't even get decent drinking water," Ball said.

A lot of people in Martin County won't drink the tap water. A clerk at the local Save A Lot supermarket estimated that about three out of four people she checks out are buying bottled water.

"We drink nothing but bottled water," resident Josie Delong said. "I even put bottled water in my kids' bathroom when they brush their teeth."

Delong said the water has long had a chemical smell, and she worries that it might be contributing to her digestive health problems. She lives in Warfield, which is across a ridgeline from Martin County's water intake on the Tug Fork River near Inez, the county seat. Because the aging pumps have to send water over the hill, Warfield sees a lot of service interruptions.

Any increase in demand can cause a cascade of problems for the fragile system of aging pipes and pumps. For example, on nights when the temperature drops below freezing, many people in poorly insulated homes will leave their taps slightly open, to make sure pipes don't freeze. One winter day in 2015, that was enough to drain the system's water tanks and leave people without water.

Hammond said water managers would sometimes have to shut off service to residents at night just to make sure there would be enough water the next day for schools to operate.

The water system here was built in the 1960s, and state public service commission records indicate the county has not invested in appropriate maintenance over the years. Like most coal-producing counties, Martin County relied heavily on revenue from taxes on coal extraction. Coal's decline has had an enormous impact on the county budget.

Judge Kelly Callaham, the top elected official in Martin County, said the local government has been forced to make a lot of cutbacks, since the county is now getting less than a quarter of the tax revenue it had as recently as three years before.

"If somebody'd looked at me when we was getting $800,000 a quarter and said, 'Judge, you're not gonna get but $150,000 three years down the road,' I'd say, 'You're crazy, man,'" Callaham said. "But that's what happened."

Critics, including newspaper editor Gary Ball, said that the county's leadership should have been better prepared for the industry's inevitable downturn, and he points out some questionable spending choices. The county put millions into a new government center building, for example—money that Ball said could have been better spent on the county's water system.

"People just aren't trustful of their political leaders," Ball said. "And when you think about it, the leaders haven't given them a whole lot to win that trust."

In any event, the drastic loss of coal income, coupled with the declining population, makes it harder to pay for improvements, which have now become critical. Hammond said there isn't enough money to make the kinds of fixes that are really needed, and the patches being made are short-term at best.

"If you have a hole already, it's just going to get bigger," he said.

After the Ohio Valley ReSource first reported on Martin County's water woes in 2017, it became a national symbol of rural America's neglected infrastructure. The resulting media attention no doubt motivated some attempts by political leaders to get more funding into the county.

But even with promised federal grants, the long-term repairs required a rate increase. A report compiled in 2019 by a citizens' group and the Appalachian Citizens' Law Center, a nonprofit law firm, found that of the 141 districts regulated by the state's public service commission, Martin County has the eighth-highest average water bill.[4]

The Environmental Protection Agency has guidelines to help water districts price water at an affordable level. Water is considered unaffordable when it costs more than 2.5 percent of household income.

According to the law center report, 46 percent of all Martin County residents face water costs that exceed those guidelines. Martin County's poorest residents, those earning less than $10,000 per year, pay as much as 6.5 percent of their income toward water bills.

"When you're making less than $10,000 a year, pretty much everything is unaffordable," ACLC attorney Mary Cromer said.

As the people of Martin County struggle with water bills, the county is cracking down on delinquent payments. In a system with just 3,500 customers, managers issued three hundred disconnect notices in just one month, Cromer found. The county sheriff has gone so far as to arrest a resident for stealing water by routing a pipe to his house around the meter.

Cromer said water managers and political leaders need to think bigger. "People need to be rethinking how we're designing water systems and how we're looking at rates and how we're funding infrastructure repairs," she said.

There was something else about the water bills that had some residents upset. For years the bills would sometimes be accompanied by a notice that the water had exceeded maximum allowable levels for some contaminants. The notices warned that long-term exposure can increase the risk of health problems, especially for the elderly, infants, and anyone with a compromised immune system.

The contaminants in question are chemical by-products of the disinfection treatment at the water plant, as chlorine interacts with organic molecules in the source water. Those organics might be algae or decaying leaves or, more likely than not in this area, improperly treated sewage.

Some communities in Martin County and many other parts of central Appalachia still lack adequate wastewater infrastructure, which means sewage often gets "straight-piped" into the nearest stream.

Gail Brion directs the University of Kentucky's Environmental Research and Training Laboratories and has worked on water treatment issues for decades. She calls the amount of sewage in this region's watershed "as close as I could come to Third World conditions without a passport."

More sewage in the water source means more chlorine is needed to treat it, which means more potentially harmful disinfection byproducts in drinking water. A report by the Environmental Working Group, an advocacy organization, used EPA data to identify hundreds of examples of this sort of contamination around the region, especially among small water systems that draw their water from surface sources.

Before taking her position in Kentucky, Brion worked at the EPA. She said the EPA and other agencies used to provide a lot more federal money, in the form of direct grants, for systems like Martin County's. But beginning with the Reagan administration, there was a fundamental shift in how the federal government approached water infrastructure funding.

"That money has now become a revolving loan fund that has to be paid back," she said. "And when you can't pay for your services to begin with, how are you going to pay back a loan to make those services better?"

The Kentucky Public Service Commission has ordered Martin County to hire an outside management company to run the district's water system, and residents worry that will bring yet another rate increase.

In its order, the PSC's chairman Michael Schmitt called the district's condition "grim and desperate." Residents of Martin County are, he wrote, "captive customers of what most certainly has been, over the last two decades, the most poorly operated water district in the state of Kentucky."

Martin County may now be the most notorious of rural water systems, but it is by no means alone in the types of problems it faces. In 2019, the Kentucky PSC was also investigating other water utilities struggling with water-loss rates similar to Martin County's. A PSC spokesman called them "the leaky eleven."

All across Appalachian coal country, communities face the combination of dwindling population, declining federal funding, aging infrastructure, and a collapsing tax base. The most recent report from the American Society of Civil Engineers found that Kentucky's drinking water infrastructure needs $8.2 billion in investment, an increase of 33 percent over five years. Ohio needs more than $13 billion, and West Virginia about $1.4 billion.[5]

The ReSource team analyzed EPA data and found that of the more than two thousand public water systems in Kentucky, Ohio, and West Virginia, 12 percent are either considered "serious violators" or had formal enforcement actions within the previous five years. The EPA defines "serious violators" as public water systems with "unresolved serious, multiple, and/or continuing violations."[6]

This is the state of affairs in a region seeking to reinvent itself. Many communities that now face the almost unimaginably large task of diversifying local economies and attracting new industry also face this question: How do you bring in people and businesses if you can't promise them a clean glass of water?

And that's just one of the water problems here.

"WE'RE BAPTISTS, and the water is very important to us here," Woodrow Nichols said.

Nichols was pastor of Union United Baptist Church in Martin County at the time, in March 2001. At a Sunday service that spring, Nichols asked from the pulpit for a show of hands: How many people had been baptized in Wolf Creek, which winds just behind the church? Hands went up from pews all around.

"This is our way of life," Nichols said. Unlike many other churches that had built small indoor pools, or baptistries, for the ceremony, Nichols said his congregation preferred the old way. "We could afford a baptistry any time we wanted it, but we choose the creek. We like that."

He said there was something special about the stream: the trees lining the banks, minnows darting around your feet. It connected people to God's creation at the very moment they took the quick, backward plunge into a new life.

But there would be no baptisms in Wolf Creek on that Sunday, or many Sundays to follow. Six months earlier, on October 11, 2000, a coal slurry impoundment operated by Martin County Coal, a Massey Energy subsidiary, gave way, sending some 300 million gallons of sludge pouring down Wolf Creek and another stream and into the Tug Fork River.[7] The massive pulse of thick black slurry continued downstream to the Big Sandy River, then to the Ohio River, darkening water, killing aquatic life, and forcing towns to close drinking-water intakes all along the way.

The impoundment was one of hundreds of such sludge ponds associated with large surface mines, called mountaintop-removal mines, many of them holding millions of gallons of toxic, semiliquid slurry left over from processing coal.

The collapse of the Martin County sludge pond carried echoes of one of the largest mass fatality events in the region's mining history: the Buffalo Creek disaster in West Virginia. In 1972, the earthen dam of a mine's sludge pond gave way in heavy rains, sending a deadly torrent down the narrow valley, wiping out entire communities and killing 125 people.

The Buffalo Creek disaster forced tighter regulation and enforcement on mining companies as they constructed the dams for sludge ponds. But in Martin County, a subsequent government investigation found, the Massey-owned mining company had built its sludge pond on top of a labyrinth of older mining tunnels in the hill the company was now dismantling from the top. The rock layer between the bottom of the sludge pond and the roof of the old mining tunnels gave way. The result was like pulling the plug in a tub.

Slurry raced through the abandoned mine tunnels, eventually shooting out into the valleys below. Some residents said that it was a near miracle that the rushing waste found more than one exit. Had it all emptied into just one place, they said, this could well have been an event on par with Buffalo Creek.

As it was, the thick black sludge covered huge areas, creeping up to some homes. Months later, Wolf Creek still ran slate-gray behind Nichols's church. Running a stick through the sandy bottom brought up fresh clouds of the sludge, now buried in the creek bed. Heavy equipment growled in the distance, part of an ongoing multimillion-dollar cleanup. At the time the EPA called it the worst environmental disaster to ever strike the southeast.

The agency had to revise that statement just eight years later, when another massive slurry spill hit the town of Kingston in eastern Tennessee, not far from Knoxville. More than a billion gallons of toxic sludge spilled out from a TVA power plant waste pond, surrounding homes and tainting the Clinch and Emory Rivers. The cleanup took years, and many workers exposed to the slurry fell ill with rashes, lung diseases, and cancers. In 2018, a jury found that the engineering firm that hired those workers had failed to protect them from exposure to the many toxic components in the sludge, including radium and arsenic. By then, many of the ill workers were already dead.[8]

The Tennessee and Kentucky sludge spills represented risks from both ends of coal's fuel cycle—the dig and the burn—and serve as reminders of just how thoroughly polluting coal is from start to finish.

The sludge at Martin County was a by-product of mining coal. Many mountaintop-removal operations and other large surface mines include a system for washing the dirt and rock from the coal before it is shipped off. This produces a large amount of liquid waste, which is held in giant slurry impoundments. Mining companies typically reuse the water, employing chemical additives to make the solid particles sink to the bottom of the impoundment, resulting in a sludge the consistency of pudding.

In addition to catastrophic failures, slurry impoundments and coal treatment facilities frequently release "blackwater" into waterways. Alpha Resources, the company that later assumed control of the Massey mines, was an especially flagrant blackwater polluter. In 2014, Alpha agreed to pay $27.5 million for thousands of permit violations. The EPA called it "the largest penalty in history" under the applicable section of the Clean Water Act.[9]

The sludge that spilled from the TVA power plant property in Tennessee, on the other hand, was a by-product of *burning* coal. The ash left over after burning coal is one of the largest sources of industrial waste in the country. The EPA says that in a typical year, coal-fired power plants produced about 110 million tons of coal ash. Hundreds of waste ponds and landfills dot the landscape throughout Appalachia and the Midwest, often along rivers where power plants are located. Burning concentrates the cornucopia of toxic elements found in small amounts in coal; the ash frequently contains arsenic, cadmium, cobalt, lead, mercury, and radium.

In 2018, the ReSource and partner station WFPL analyzed data from groundwater monitoring wells near ash disposal sites in Ohio, Kentucky, and West Virginia.[10] The EPA required electric utility companies to supply the monitoring information under rules developed during the Obama administration. This was the first batch of public data. Our analysis showed that most of the coal ash disposal sites were leaking contaminants into groundwater. At several sites, hazardous compounds were found in groundwater at levels that far exceeded federal drinking water standards.

In Kentucky, for example, groundwater monitors at seven of fourteen waste sites found arsenic at levels that exceeded federal drinking water standards. Tests at three sites showed radium levels above drinking water standards.

Utility companies and state environmental officials said there was no imminent threat to public health. The groundwater monitoring wells that produced the data were on company property, and there were not yet indications that the contamination had reached any waterways or drinking water sources. But environmental advocates worry that those contaminants could threaten human health and the environment, and they say changes to the coal ash rules made by the Trump administration will create loopholes for utility companies to delay or avoid cleanup.

Even coal mines that have been idled or abandoned for decades can continue to pollute streams and rivers. Throughout coal mining country you will see otherwise lovely mountain streams that run a peculiar rusty orange. Rocks are often stained with a slimy substance locals call "yellow boy" and in many such streams very little above the bacterial level lives in the water.

It's the result of pollution called acid mine drainage, or AMD. It's estimated that about five thousand miles of streams are polluted by AMD in Pennsylvania and West Virginia alone. Many of the rock layers surrounding coal seams contain sulfur-rich minerals such as pyrite, or fool's gold. When mining exposes the rock, water trickling through kicks off an almost never-ending chemical reaction that produces sulfuric acid and iron. The iron stains the streambeds orange and the acid kills off most of what had evolved to live in the stream for millennia before mining arrived there.

AMD can be mitigated, often with long troughs of lime or other base minerals to counter the acidity. The costs frequently fall on taxpayers, and the treatment must go on for as long as the rocks continue to produce sulfur and the hills continue to flow with water. In other words, forever.

CONCERNS ABOUT STRIP MINING are nearly as old as the practice itself. Eastern Kentucky author Harry Caudill opened his seminal 1963 book *Night Comes to the Cumberlands* with an indictment of his region's chief industry.

> Coal has always cursed the land in which it lies. When men begin to wrest it from the earth, it leaves a legacy of foul streams, hideous slag heaps and polluted air. It peoples this transformed land with blind and crippled men and with widows and orphans. It is an extractive industry which takes all away and restores nothing. It mars but never beautifies. It corrupts but never purifies.[11]

And that was written when strip-mining operations were still relatively small.

Some three decades later, a new practice called mountaintop removal took surface mining to an exponentially greater level in Appalachia. Entire hilltops are blasted away and massive equipment dumps the waste rock and dirt into nearby "valley fills." The explosions and earthmoving put giant clouds of dust into the air, and the flattened hills and filled-in valleys disrupt ecosystems and leach chemicals into streams and groundwater.

People living near these operations have long suspected the practice is to blame for health problems ranging from asthma to skin conditions to cancer, all of which seemed too common for communities so small. But proving the link is another matter.

In 2006, Dr. Michael Hendryx arrived at West Virginia University as a professor of public health. His research focused on health disparities for disadvantaged populations. When he arrived in West Virginia he soon started to hear the concerns about the health impacts of mountaintop removal. He tried to read up on the science behind the matter, but there was not much to read.

"I looked at the literature and found nothing had been done in the United States on public health problems related to mining," he said. So he decided to study it himself.

Many of his colleagues were skeptical. He was told that health problems would be due to other issues common in coalfield communities. But Hendryx used statistical analyses to control for issues such as poverty and smoking and found that there was still something more that was causing poor health outcomes.

"I can literally remember the very first study, hitting the run button on my computer, and seeing that, yes, there was something there," he said. "I was surprised!"

Over the next few years, he and colleagues published peer-reviewed work that linked large-scale surface mining to a variety of health issues for those living nearby, including increased rates of cancer, lung disease, and birth defects.

His study in the *Journal of Toxicology and Environmental Health* linked life near mountaintop removal mines to higher rates of hospitalization for hypertension and chronic obstructive pulmonary disease (COPD).[12]

The *American Journal of Public Health* published Hendryx's analysis expanding that to include cardiopulmonary disease, lung disease, and kidney disease.[13] Another study by his colleagues in the *Journal of Community Health* connected surface mining to increased cancer risks in nearby communities, and in the journal *Environmental Science and Technology* he linked lung cancers to exposure from dust from mountaintop removal.[14]

In *Public Health Reports*, Hendryx estimated the economic costs of lives shortened by the health effects he had identified. The conclusion: "The human cost of Appalachian coal mining outweighs its economic benefits."[15]

The response from government was not what Hendryx expected. "I was naïve, and thought that maybe the evidence would speak for itself," he said with a wry laugh. "But I've learned that's not how things work in the coalfields of West Virginia."

Bill Raney is the president of the West Virginia Coal Association. When asked about Hendryx, he described him as "anti-mining." Raney said he doesn't trust Hendryx's research, and he thinks it ignores a bigger health concern: the loss of mining jobs, which has fed into a wide range of health issues across the region's coalfields. "When they don't have a job, then health suffers," Raney said. It is of course possible that both things are true.

The mining industry sponsored its own studies to scrutinize Hendryx's research. Much of the criticism argued that influences of smoking, obesity, and poverty were really behind the region's health problems. One critic went so far as to argue that Hendryx's findings were not reliable because they did not account for "consanguinity"—the scientific term for inbreeding.

One coal company filed a request for every document, email, and scrap of paper connected to years of Hendryx's research. "A fishing expedition," Hendryx said, "to make me waste time."

In 2015, Hendryx was called to testify before a congressional committee, where he didn't exactly get a warm reception from John Fleming, a Louisiana Republican. Fleming described Hendryx's research as less scientific than a fifth-grade science project. "You should be embarrassed to be here with a study like this," Fleming said.

But within the world of scientific research, Hendryx's work was gaining notice and inspiring others to take a closer look at mountaintop-removal mining. In a 2010 edition of the prestigious journal *Science*, several prominent researchers called for a moratorium on mountaintop removal.[16] Local residents also wanted firmer answers about the health effects the studies had found, and West Virginia officials asked the US Department of the Interior to act.

In the waning months of the Obama administration, Interior's Office of Surface Mining Reclamation and Enforcement funded a study by the National Academy of Sciences to review the health effects of mountaintop removal.[17] "West Virginia asked us in the federal government for help," OSMRE director Joe Pizarchik said in a statement. "So we brought the National Academy of Sciences on board because they are one of the world's most reputable scientific organizations."

Michael Hendryx called it a positive step. "They are at least recognizing that there's an issue," he said at the time. By then he had left West Virginia for a position at the University of Indiana, Bloomington.

Given his experience with coalfield politics, he was wary. "I'm going to wait and see what happens."

The National Academy set about selecting a committee of twelve independent experts on issues including mining engineering, epidemiology, public health, and environmental medicine. The committee arranged for four town hall–style meetings in Appalachia to gather information over the course of their two-year study.

Then came election day. About six months after President Trump took office, his Interior Department sent a letter to the National Academy instructing it to "cease all activities . . . effective immediately" regarding the mining study. The letter said this was "largely as a result of our changing budget situation."

For those familiar with how the National Academy operates, the Trump administration's move was alarming.

"I've never seen a study halted in the middle," said Andrew Rosenberg, director of the Center for Science and Democracy at the Union of Concerned Scientists, a Washington-based advocacy group. Rosenberg took part in numerous National Academy studies during his service in the National Oceanic and Atmospheric Administration. He said he was skeptical about the Interior Department's reason for stopping the study.

"They have a budget, it's a continuing resolution from last year, there wasn't a provision that says, 'Oh, we're cutting your granting program,'" he said. "The money was well known; this is a two-year study in its second year. So, you know, that's a very thin excuse."

Using the Freedom of Information Act, the ReSource sought Interior Department records relating to the decision to halt the study. Eight months later Interior responded with documents that had largely been redacted. Reporting by the *Pacific Standard* found Interior officials met with coal company executives shortly before pulling the plug on the National Academy's work.[18]

Duke University ecologist Emily Bernhardt, who has been studying the effects of mountaintop removal on water quality, said she had hoped the National Academy's work would help resolve some of the lingering questions.

"I think the public health outcomes are pretty clear," she said. What was still unclear was exactly why those living near the mines had so much poorer health. "What is the most likely route of exposure? And that's one of the reasons this Academy summary was going to be so important."

At a later congressional hearing on the matter, Michael McCawley, professor of environmental health at West Virginia University, pointed to what he called strong evidence linking the mining practice to a variety of negative health effects. McCawley said his work on air quality near mines also shows high levels of fine particulate matter, which is known to present health hazards. He testified that the science on the health effects should now be considered more than simply correlative. "They should be considered causal."

McCawley said he thought Trump's Interior officials knew that the National Academy would reach a similar conclusion.

"I think they believed that the study was going to come out with evidence that supported banning mountaintop mining—that they knew what the evidence was," he said.

Donna Branham of Lenore, West Virginia, was among the coal community residents who told the committee they were hoping the National Academy would finally address concerns about effects on air and water quality. When people learned that the study had been stopped, Branham told lawmakers, "We felt abandoned; we felt as if our lives didn't matter."

"THE COAL MINE at the top of the ridge here, they let off a blast maybe around two in the afternoon. My windows will rattle, my dishes will shake," Jason Walker said. Walker lives in Wyoming County, in southern West Virginia, not far from a mountaintop-removal coal mine operated by a company called Dynamic Energy. It was certainly dynamic for Walker. "You'll actually feel the blast."

Jason Walker of West Virginia inspects the thousand-gallon tank he uses to store water he draws from a nearby stream. His family's well failed after large-scale coal mining started nearby. "I just really want clean water," he said. "It's not a whole lot to ask for, either."

Walker, age thirty-one, lives next door to his mother, Sherry Walker, and for years the two Walker households shared a water well. But after the mining started, they noticed changes. Rust-colored residue accumulated in the water filtration system, a sign of high iron content.

Walker was diagnosed with a chronic inflammation of the gastrointestinal tract, something medical research has linked to elevated iron levels in water. The Walkers had their water tested. The lab found the well water had high levels of manganese and levels of iron far higher than the EPA's recommended limit. Over time, the Walkers' well became unusable, then dried up altogether.

Now, Walker said, he spends $50 a month on bottled water, which he uses for drinking and cooking. He also spends about three hours each week standing by the small stream that runs near his house, pumping creek water into a thousand-gallon, heavy-duty plastic tank. This is his new water supply.

"You have to catch the creek at the right time, when it's clear," Walker said. "Whatever the creek looks like is what you're going to pump, and that's going to pump right into your house."

In 2016, Walker and several of his neighbors sued Dynamic Energy, blaming the company for their health problems. But the judge ruled that lawyers for the families could not prove conclusively that pollutants in the residents' drinking water were the result of the mining. They lost. The owner of Dynamic Energy at the time, Jim Justice, was elected West Virginia's governor that year. Justice's son now controls the mining company.

Walker said the flare-ups of his illness quieted when he switched to bottled water, and he's become accustomed to the challenges of pumping and treating his own water from the stream.

He doesn't want to leave the holler where he grew up and where his father is buried. Even if he did want to leave, he probably couldn't. His property value tanked when the well dried up.

"I just really want clean water," he said. "It's not a whole lot to ask for, either. It's really not."

6.
Tough Choices in Belmont County

November 2018 had already brought a light dusting of snow to the upper Ohio Valley, and the hundred or so people filing into the auditorium at Shadyside High School were shaking off the cold and shedding coats and hats.

They'd come out that evening from nearby towns around Belmont County, Ohio, from just across the river, in Moundsville, West Virginia, and from the steel town of Wheeling just to the north. They were there for a public hearing hosted by Ohio's environmental regulators.

Officially, the focus of the hearing was a nearly three-hundred-page, densely technical air quality permit for a proposed new facility along the banks of the Ohio, just a few miles from the school.[1]

But everyone gathered understood that much more was at stake. The permit was one more small step toward a massive, multibillion-dollar buildout of chemical plants that would turn the petroleum products trapped in rock deep beneath them into plastics that would go around the world.

The abundance of natural gas unleashed by hydraulic fracturing of shale, or fracking, may soon fuel a new petrochemical industry in the upper Ohio Valley, with all the economic gains and environmental risks that entails. It was a crossroads moment for the people who live here, with implications for the entire planet.

"It is a project such as this that will revitalize the Ohio Valley," Glenn Giffin said in his time at the microphone. Giffin is president of Wheeling's Local 141 of the electrical workers' union, the IBEW. Wheeling was the center of a steel industry that once employed nearly twenty thousand people along West Virginia's northern panhandle, and the city still struggles to rebound from the industry's sharp decline. Giffin and other supporters see a potential economic boom at hand.

The construction work alone for such a large-scale plant would put electricians from his local to work, with the promise of six hundred more jobs to follow.

But Belmont County resident Jill Hunkler said she sees this plant as the beginning of something else: an environmental nightmare.

"We want better options than a massive petrochemical plant," Hunkler told the audience.

Fracking for natural gas has already transformed much of the region, for good and ill—bringing pollution, disruption, land disputes, and anxiety, as well as jobs and new revenue that have boosted many struggling local economies. But despite steady demand from electric utilities to fire new gas-powered generators, gas prices have stayed low. A glut of gas and the industry's natural tendency to boom-and-bust cycles undercut efforts to build a more stable prosperity from the wealth of shale gas.

Economic development officials and industry leaders have a one-word solution for that: plastics.

Natural gas in its pure methane form, CH_4—four hydrogen atoms around a central carbon atom—is the product now displacing coal as the fuel of choice for many electric power plants. But that is not the only product of the fracking process. Frack wells also bring up a host of "wet gas" products like ethane, also called natural gas liquids, or NGLs. The famed Marcellus Shale layer beneath much of northern Appalachia, and another even deeper rock layer beneath it called the Utica Shale formation, are rich in these NGLs. These products can fetch a higher market price because the petrochemical industry can turn them into plastics and resins.

It's a big job to turn these NGLs into something manufacturing facilities can use, and that job starts with something called an ethane "cracker." These large facilities superheat ethane and "crack" apart the molecule to produce ethylene, the ur-chemical that manufacturers use to create plastics, resins, adhesives, and many other products that have become essential parts of modern life. Ethylene is probably the most commonly manufactured petrochemical.

That's the type of facility proposed for Belmont County: a cracker plant, to turn the gas liquids from rock layers into an estimated 1.5 million tons of ethylene a year.

A few years ago, the Thailand-based company PTT Global Chemical began scouting the Ohio Valley for a location for a cracker plant. JobsOhio, a private economic development corporation created by then governor John Kasich, worked closely with the company.

Matt Cybulski is director of energy and chemicals for JobsOhio. He said the group helped PTT select the Belmont County location and put together an incentive package. That included site remediation of an old coal-fired power plant, now shuttered, along a horseshoe bend in the Ohio River near a small community called Dilles Bottom.

A few homes dot the unincorporated hamlet. There's a cemetery and what used to be a post office, now closed. But in 2018, PTT and a South Korean partner purchased five hundred acres of land here, and little Dilles Bottom could soon be the hub of a giant new industrial center.

"Once the plant is built, you have hundreds of good-paying jobs that are operating the plant," Cybulski said. "So we see this as a long-term economic benefit for the local community and the region."

Energy analysts say the cracker plant in Belmont County could have far-reaching impacts for the entire region.

"It's going to create some real momentum," industry consultant Taylor Robinson said, explaining the chain of petroleum and manufacturing infrastructure and companies that would soon follow.

"You're going to need to have enough wells producing the gas," Robinson said. "Then you're going to have to have more gas-processing facilities that will separate the ethane out. And then you need storage. Of course you need pipelines between all these things. It's a complex supply chain that needs to be built for forty years."

A 2017 report from the US Department of Energy projects NGL production to increase over 700 percent by 2023, compared to levels ten years before. The report says, "Forecasts for production over the decades to come highlight the opportunity for additional investments across the NGL supply chain."[2]

If the PTT project is built, the Ohio Valley would also need to develop massive underground storage areas for natural gas products.

"That is extremely important when you start adding multiple crackers, because as you can imagine, there's several steps to get the ethane to the plants," energy consultant Robinson said. "You need storage along the way, and those storage caverns are a key enabler to have enough flexibility to keep these crackers running twenty-four seven, three hundred and sixty-five days a year."

A company called Energy Storage Ventures is developing the Mountaineer NGL Storage project to meet some of that demand. When completed, the project would store 2 million barrels of ethane, butane, and propane in four underground salt caverns on a two-hundred-acre site, about one mile north of Clarington, Ohio, along the Ohio River.

But even that would fall short of the NGL storage needed to support the scale of production that boosters here envision.

Another high-profile public-private project in the works is the Appalachia Storage and Trading Hub. The hub would make use of underground salt formations to store up to 10 million barrels of materials. It was to be paid for as part of an investment by China's largest partially state-owned energy company, China Energy. President Trump's visit to China in 2017 culminated in a ceremony in Beijing's Great Hall of the People to mark US-China business deals that would bring some $250 billion of Chinese investment to the United States.[3]

About $84 billion of that was promised for Appalachian natural gas deals. A memorandum of understanding with state officials from West Virginia called for facilities to be constructed over twenty years to generate power and support a petrochemical industry, including the gas storage hub.

In late 2017, Governor Jim Justice of West Virginia told an audience at a town hall event sponsored by WSAZ television that the project could start within a year. "It would not surprise me, within my ten-month window of today, to see shovels in the ground," he said.

But more than two years later, the project is still just a proposal and the Chinese deal seems to be collateral damage from Trump's trade war.

Brian Anderson, now head of the Energy Department's National Energy Technology Laboratory, once led West Virginia University's Energy Institute, where he had close contact with Chinese energy representatives. Anderson said they were scouting potential locations for projects. In the summer of 2018, Anderson was scheduled to join his Chinese counterparts at the Northeast US Petrochemical Construction Conference in Pittsburgh to officially announce the first set of projects.

But the Chinese partners didn't show up.

"With the bilateral tensions between the US and China, the executive-level officials from China Energy felt it was not an appropriate time for them to come for an official visit," Anderson said.

The storage hub developers are looking to another source of funding—the US government. The project cleared a hurdle early in 2018, with initial approval for a $1.9 billion loan guarantee from the US Department of Energy.

Environmental groups posted signs in Shadyside, Ohio, where a proposed facility will convert ethane from natural gas into petrochemical products. The plant promises jobs but also the threat of pollution. "We want jobs that won't kill us," an organizer said.

ON THE AFTERNOON before the Ohio air permit hearing, a small group went door-to-door in a neighborhood of Moundsville, West Virginia, sharing information about the proposed cracker plant and what it could mean for the area's environment.

Barbara Mew was powering through biting cold and wind-driven flurries.

"I think I've pushed through to the other side," she said, laughing. "It's not cold anymore."

She worries about the pollution the huge plant will emit into the air and water. The draft air permit under consideration that day estimated the cracker will release almost four hundred tons of volatile organic compounds each year, as well as pumping out greenhouse gases.

"It's just an environmental nightmare from top to bottom," Mew said. "There are really no upsides to it."

Leatra Harper, managing director of the nonprofit Freshwater Accountability Project, which organized the canvassing, said the volunteers knocked on hundreds of doors and found most people have questions about the plant's public health impacts. One common concern is that the Ohio Valley could turn into the next "cancer alley."

The term refers to the huge, heavily polluted belt of chemical manufacturing facilities in Louisiana. For decades, most of this kind of petrochemical manufacturing in the United States has taken place along the Gulf Coast, and host communities have long suffered disproportionate levels of disease.

"I don't understand why fossil fuel extraction is the only kind of job this area is offered," Harper said. "We want jobs that won't kill us."

At the hearing that evening, opponents said the proposed air permit does not do enough to protect public health, despite assurances from agency officials that the plant would install top-of-the-line technologies to limit emissions.

According to the permit, nitrogen oxide and carbon dioxide emissions will be continuously monitored, but other pollutants will only be tested intermittently. Many people expressed concerns that the company building the facility, PTT, is not required to monitor for pollutants along the fence line with neighboring properties or to actively track what is being emitted from the plant. They are also concerned that the one air quality monitor that is installed in the county would not be sufficient to alert local communities to any pollution above permitted levels. Many asked for a health impact assessment to determine the potential public health effects of the facility.

Activists also asked that the Ohio EPA conduct a cumulative assessment of air emissions from all the other natural gas industry infrastructure that would be spurred by the cracker plant. As boosters have pointed out, the PTT plant would be part of a much larger web of gas drilling, delivery, and processing infrastructure and facilities.

But the state regulatory system is not equipped for that kind of comprehensive measure of potential environmental or health effects. Ohio EPA hearing officer Kristopher Weiss said the agency's jurisdiction is fairly narrow, and requires the agency to take action on individual permits within a set period of time.

If the PTT plant spurs additional developments, he said, Ohio EPA would evaluate each new project on an individual basis.

So while proponents sell the facility on a promise of jobs and revenue from future petrochemical development, there is no means to assess the cumulative impact of that development—no true risk-benefit analysis of what is really being proposed.

On the outskirts of Shadyside, not far from where the new PTT plant would be built, retired public health practitioner Susan Brown sat in Van Dyne's, a diner that's locally famous for its all-you-can-eat spaghetti. She said she worries about what will happen to her community.

"The fracking plant came in. Then we're talking about the cracker plant. They're talking about the underground tanks," she said, sipping an unsweetened tea. She's concerned that her town is approaching a point where it will be "an area that nobody wants to live."

Brown says most people she talks to about the cracker plant feel like it's a done deal. Still, she thinks it's important to speak out.

THE CUMULATIVE IMPACT of plastics production on this scale goes well beyond the surrounding community. It can also create problems for the world's oceans and atmosphere.

On a brisk May morning, Lakshmi Narayanan and Myrna Dominguez are bumping along rough country roads in West Virginia's Wetzel County, just southeast of where the new ethane cracker plant would be built, and right in the middle of the frack drilling that would supply the new plastics industry.

The two women are activists who work with communities dealing firsthand with the world's proliferation of plastics.

Dominguez works for the Philippines-based group Pangisda, a network of people in Southeast Asia who make their livings from fishing. She describes plastic choking Manila Bay, which was once one of the country's most productive natural fish nurseries.

"These plastics are polluting our oceans, our fishing grounds, especially the municipal fishing grounds, which is the main source of livelihood of small fisherfolk, and this is small plastics or single-use plastics," she said—plastic bags, straws, shampoo bottles everywhere.

Fisherfolk often have to travel miles out from their port to catch fish, and when they do, they find fish full of plastic. Dominguez has come to this corner of Appalachia as part of a fact-finding and exchange mission organized by a coalition of environmental groups called Break Free From Plastic. They want to see where some of those plastics might one day originate.

Fracking's effect on this rural landscape is not hard to spot. The infrastructure required to tap into the natural gas stored deep in the Marcellus Shale involves a sprawling network of drilling pads, pipelines, compressor stations, and trucks—lots of heavy trucks. Fleets of trucks haul drilling water in and brine water out. Other trucks are laden with steel pipe, spewing diesel exhaust as they barrel by.

Narayanan cofounded KKPKP, a trade union of self-employed waste pickers in India. She works to win protections for these workers, often illiterate and very poor, who do the backbreaking work every day of separating paper, metal, glass, and plastic for recycling.

Increasingly, she says, the waste pickers are finding new kinds of plastics, like flexible plastic packaging. It's hard to recycle and not valuable enough for the pickers to collect. But it's there and someone has to deal with it. Narayanan argues that manufacturers are creating new, lighter plastics because it is good for their image and bottom line, but they are content to let India's poor sort out their disposal.

"The manufacturers are sending them out because there are no costs that they are taking," Narayanan said. "If they had to take the cost of collecting it after it was used, and of ensuring that it goes through its chain of sorting, and transport, and processing, and then recycling, it would probably be unaffordable."

Later that afternoon, after seeing well pads, compressor stations, and forty-two-inch steel pipe being laid into a hillside ripped bare of trees, Narayanan said she sees a whole other side to plastics.

"It's horrifying how a single product can begin its life causing so much destruction and end its life with the same level of destruction."

Around the world, people are growing alarmed about plastic pollution in the ocean. Reports of plastic garbage patches in the eyes of oceanic gyres and grisly images of marine wildlife choking on our disposable wrappers, straws, and convenience items have galvanized a movement to reduce plastic waste. But the very act of creating plastics in the manner proposed for the Ohio Valley may well do just as much harm to the environment.

Plastics production is very carbon-intensive, with every step of the process emitting greenhouse gases. The ethane cracker planned for Belmont County would produce carbon dioxide emissions equivalent to an additional 365,000 cars on the road. Another ethane cracker plant already underway in Pennsylvania will release an annual 2.2 million tons of carbon dioxide, about the same amount as 467,000 vehicles.[4]

In the April 2019 issue of the journal *Nature Climate Change*, scientists at UC Santa Barbara's Bren School of Environmental Science and Management published what they called "the first global assessment of the life cycle of greenhouse gas emissions from all plastics."[5]

They found that, with the expansion of plastics manufacturing planned for places like the upper Ohio Valley, global plastics production will become a major climate change threat. Their results show that the global life cycle of greenhouse gas emissions from conventional plastics is now equivalent to 1.7 gigatons of CO_2. They project that we are on a path for that to grow to 6.5 gigatons by 2050.

If the current growth trend for petroleum-based plastics continues, they found, the emissions from plastics could reach 15 percent of the global carbon budget by midcentury. In other words, if we are to achieve the greenhouse gas emission reductions that scientists say we need in order to avoid the most dangerous warming, plastics alone would take up about a sixth of all allowable emissions.

The scientists also explored ways that plastics could be made less harmful to the atmosphere.

The most promising methods were to make plastics from plant-based materials instead of petroleum feedstocks and to manufacture them using renewable energy rather than by burning natural gas.

But of course that is the opposite of what's proposed now in the upper Ohio Valley, which is premised entirely on the use of abundant shale gas and NGLs.

At about the same time that study was published, a coalition of environmental organizations produced a report with a similar goal, to measure the climate impacts of society's growing need for plastics.

"We wanted to better understand the implications of that massive new buildout of plastics infrastructure for the global climate," coauthor Carroll Muffett said. Muffett is president and CEO of the nonprofit Center for International Environmental Law. "Ninety-nine percent of what goes into plastics is fossil fuels, and their climate impacts actually start at the wellhead and the drill pad."

The report estimates that the production and incineration of plastic in 2019 added more than 850 million metric tons of greenhouse gases to the atmosphere, the equivalent of building 189 new coal-fired power plants. The facilities planned for the upper Ohio Valley are part of a larger expansion of plastic production around the world. If that happens, the report predicts that by 2030 emissions from plastics could reach 1.34 gigatons per year, equivalent to about 295 coal power plants.[6]

"This petrochemical buildout is a key driver of plastic's contribution to climate impacts, now and in the future," Muffett said.

In a statement, the trade group the American Chemistry Council said the report failed to take into account the ways that plastic products improve energy efficiency by replacing heavier, more energy-intensive materials.

"Because plastics are strong and lightweight, they help us do more with less," said Steve Russell, vice president of the group's plastics division.

But much of the demand for plastics is driven by single-use, disposable products, packaging, and wrapping—not the type of products Russell describes. A study of the potential customers for plastics points out that nearly 60 percent of polyethylene plastics and almost 40 percent of polypropylene plastics are consumed as packaging. The source of that report? The American Chemistry Council.

The plastics manufacturing boom northern Appalachia is embarking upon is a multibillion-dollar, multigenerational commitment to making plastics from fossil fuels, something that is likely to make it even harder to avoid dangerous levels of climate change.

FRACKING IS, of course, already a major source of greenhouse gases, not just from burning the fuel but from so-called fugitive emissions, a fancy term for when drilling and transmission operations leak methane, a potent greenhouse gas, into the atmosphere.

People who live near fracking operations have long lists of complaints about air and water quality, not to mention the noise from drilling and the damage and accidents caused by heavy truck traffic.

And then there is the drilling waste. Water and solids brought to the surface by fracking drills frequently contain low levels of naturally occurring radioactive materials. The gas industry produces thousands of tons of this waste, and companies throughout the Ohio Valley are constantly looking for affordable ways to get rid of it.

In 2016 in Doddridge County, in the northern part of West Virginia, petroleum engineer Tom Waltz explained the features of a new fracking operation built by Antero Resources.

"We're preparing to fracture the rock," Waltz said. "And hopefully make a decent amount of oil and gas."

He pointed to eight green sixteen-thousand-gallon aboveground storage tanks at the edge of the drilling pad. "They hold produced water that the producing wells make," he explained. "Produced water" is one form of drilling waste. It's salty water laced with chemicals, metals, and naturally occurring radioactive elements that come out of the earth, along with the gas and oil.

Later, trucks will draw water from the tanks and deliver it to either a treatment plant or disposal site. Antero is the country's eighth-largest gas drilling company and operates hundreds of sites like this, producing thousands of barrels of waste.

One way to get rid of wastewater is to inject it back into the ground, but that can lead to pollution and even earthquakes. Scientists linked tremors near Youngstown, Ohio, to an injection well, just one of dozens of seismic incidents in Ohio linked to fracking.

One of Antero's lead civil engineers at the time, Conrad Baston, said processing the wastewater—separating it into salt, sludge, and water—seemed a decent alternative to injection. A filtering system recovers much of the water, which can be reused in drilling—but even that leaves behind tons of salt and sludge from the sediment. That sludge contains the concentrated radioactive materials, which must be disposed of. That involves finding trucking and landfills equipped to handle low-level radioactive waste.

An investigation by the Center for Public Integrity found that these radioactive materials from oil and gas can become "orphan waste," because no single government agency fully manages it.[7] Instead, an inconsistent patchwork of state laws apply, and companies often shop around, looking for the most affordable disposal option.

Ohio Valley ReSource tracked a load of this hot waste as it made its way across state lines before being illegally dumped in a landfill not far from two public schools in Kentucky.[8]

Antero had contracted with a treatment company in West Virginia called Fairmont Brine to handle its liquid drilling waste. In August 2015, trucks carrying the concentrated sludge traveled from northern West Virginia to Irvine, a small town in Estill County, in eastern Kentucky. Irvine lies near the Kentucky River, where Appalachian hills give way to rolling farm country.

The trucks were headed for a municipal waste facility called Blue Ridge Landfill, which was not designed or permitted to hold low-level radioactive waste. The trucks dumped an estimated four hundred tons of the waste, just one of several such illegal shipments to Blue Ridge.

Just across Route 89 from the landfill is the home where Denny and Vivian Smith live, on property that's been in their family since the 1800s.

"This is our home place," Vivian Smith said. "This is roots for us."

From their sunporch, facing east, the Smiths can see the entrance to Blue Ridge Landfill. From their front door, facing west, they can see Estill County High School and Estill County Middle School, with a combined enrollment of about twelve hundred students. The community, the parents of schoolchildren, and the Smiths had a lot of questions.

"We are getting older, and we feel like we're kind of vulnerable to illnesses with what's going on at the landfill," Vivian Smith said.

The Environmental Protection Agency says the radioactive materials in drilling waste present real risks. Radioactive dust is potentially harmful and it would be bad if the leachate, or liquid that oozes out from the landfill, were to contaminate groundwater over time. Radioactive waste can last centuries—far longer than the engineered life span of the liners in many landfills.

A state investigation eventually resulted in fines for the landfill operator and the transportation firm. Some of the money went toward monitoring at the schools, and the landfill owners were charged with developing a mitigation plan to reduce risks from the material.

State environmental officials say they found no evidence of any contamination in the surrounding area around the landfill, and that there is little risk from managing the waste where it is. But several residents were unhappy with the state's plan to keep the radioactive waste in the Blue Ridge Landfill.

"The majority of the people I've spoken with indicate they will not have full peace of mind if it's left in place," resident Tom Bonny said. They urged the state to remove the materials and find a site designed to hold such waste.

The incident left Vivian Smith anxious about what might happen in the future and distrustful of the agencies that should have prevented this mess in the first place.

"Knowing that there was nothing going on to protect us," Smith said, "I think it's like the henhouse wasn't guarded and the fox got in."

IN 2017, Royal Dutch Shell kicked off the region's petro-plastics build-out when the company started construction on what could be the first ethane cracker to be sited beyond the Gulf Coast in twenty years. State officials offered Shell generous tax breaks to choose Monaca, Pennsylvania, about twenty-five miles downriver from Pittsburgh along the Ohio and roughly seventy-five miles from the site of the cracker plant planned for Belmont County, Ohio.

The Shell Monaca plant is expected to produce 1.6 million tons of polyethylene plastic pellets each year. About five thousand people were already employed in its design, engineering, and construction in August 2019, when President Trump toured the facility.[9]

With a backdrop of workers in company-issued yellow vests, he delivered a speech that—officially, anyway—was about energy.

As is often the case with Trump speeches, however, this one veered wildly into a range of other topics: attacks on his political opponents; asides on the size of his 2016 electoral win; complaints about the "unfair" press; and a story about his boyhood love of trucks, among other things.

When he did return to the script about energy, it was often in the form of attacks on those who would prevent the people of the Ohio Valley from using the bounty of natural gas.

"They targeted American energy for total destruction. You weren't going to be able to take anything out," Trump said. "That's our gold.

That's gold underneath their feet, and they weren't going to allow it to happen."

He criticized the Paris Agreement, the 2015 international accord to avoid dangerous levels of climate change, as something that was "good for other countries, wasn't good for us."

Trump falsely claimed that his administration had made the Pennsylvania plant and another new natural gas facility in Louisiana possible. "Without us, you would never have been able to do this." (Both facilities were fully permitted before he took office.)[10]

Trump falsely claimed that his administration had made the United States the world's "number-one energy producer." (The United States had become the top producer of petroleum in 2013, and of natural gas in 2009, according to the Energy Information Administration.)[11]

At ceremonial signing events for his various rollbacks of environmental regulations, Trump often positions himself among miners in helmets, or steelworkers in hard hats, or, as in Pennsylvania, workers in reflective safety vests.

"If they got in, your fracking is gone. Your coal is gone," Trump told the audience in Monaca.

And he made clear what kinds of jobs he thought were the only real options for the people of the Ohio Valley.

"You guys, I don't know what the hell you're going to do. You don't want to make widgets, right? Do you want to learn how to make a computer, a little tiny piece of stuff"—Trump gestured toward a beefy man nearby in the audience—"with those big, beautiful hands of yours? Take these big hands, he's going to take this little tiny part."

He pantomimed an oafish, thick-fingered attempt to work with some imagined small piece of tech equipment, to laughs from the audience. "He's going to go home: 'Alice, this is a tough job.'"

Then he let his own small hands drop and shook his head.

"No! You want to make steel, and you want to dig coal, and that's what you want to do!"

LESS THAN A MONTH after the hearing in Shadyside, the Ohio EPA issued the air permit to PTT Global for construction of the cracker plant in Belmont County.[12]

Environmental groups challenged, arguing that the state's air pollution controls were not sufficient to prevent harm to nearby communities. The groups won some concessions: the company is required to use better technology to find and repair pollution leaks, and it must create a website to share emissions data with the public.

The company had not yet made an announcement about full financing for the plant, but as Susan Brown had said earlier in the diner, it seemed to be a done deal.

In July 2019, a top official from the Department of Energy testified in front of members of the West Virginia Legislature that the federal government was making the petrochemical industry in Appalachia a priority.

"Federal efforts are strong and continue to gain momentum," Steven Winberg, the DOE's assistant secretary for fossil energy, told the lawmakers. "We believe that together we can make this Appalachian petrochemical renaissance happen for the benefit of the industry, the region, and the country."[13]

7.

Clay City Faces Diseases of Despair

DRESSED IN A black jacket and leggings, her long brown hair pulled into a ponytail, Allie looks like the college student she might have been in a different version of her life.

She sits, blinking, in a dimly lit room at a syringe exchange clinic in Lexington, Kentucky, still a little high from the heroin she shot earlier in the day. But mostly it's the news she just received that has her dazed.

Allie, twenty-four, asked to be identified only by her first name. After injecting heroin off and on for four years, she was clean for nearly a year. She then relapsed, lost her waitressing job, and lived for a while in her car. She's been a client at the Lexington-Fayette County Health Department for about six months.[1]

"The first few weeks I came I wasn't sure," she said, "that I had hep C yet."

Afraid of getting the results, she put off getting the test. But now she knows for sure.

"I actually just got the test done and it came back positive, so I just found that out five minutes ago," she said, and exhaled a long, slow breath.

She knows there is medical treatment, but the fear is clear in her eyes. The diagnosis is too big, today, for her to decide on hep C treatment or rehab. She'll keep coming back to the health department. The fifteen minutes a week she spends here is a respite from her chaotic life. People here see her. They listen.

"They don't try to change me," she said. "They don't judge me."

A hundred miles to the east, in Louisa, Kentucky, another young woman also got news that would change her life.

Given the stigma attached to addiction, Mary asked that we not use her real name. That stigma is even greater for pregnant women and mothers.[2]

Mary has struggled with an addiction that began with painkillers and progressed to heroin.

"As soon as I opened my eyes, I had to get it," Mary said. "And when I did get it, I had to think of the next way that I was going to get it."

Mary was using when she learned she was pregnant with her first child. She sought treatment, but it didn't help. The child was born dependent on opioids and went through the pains of withdrawal shortly after delivery, a condition known as neonatal abstinence syndrome, or NAS.

Infants with NAS often cry and sneeze excessively. They are sensitive to touch and easily overstimulated. They may have tremors or seizures and suffer diarrhea and weight loss. Research indicates some affected infants may experience long-term learning and behavioral problems.[3]

"To see that little boy go through that stuff, you'd think that I would, like, change my life immediately, but I didn't," Mary said. "I didn't want to believe it. I was in complete denial that it was because of my choices that he was going through that."

Mary sought treatment again, but relapsed. Then she learned she was going to have a second child.

CENTRAL APPALACHIA was ground zero for America's opioid crisis for more than a decade before it became a national epidemic. The staggering rates of addiction and overdose death in the region foretold the losses that would later affect other parts of the country.

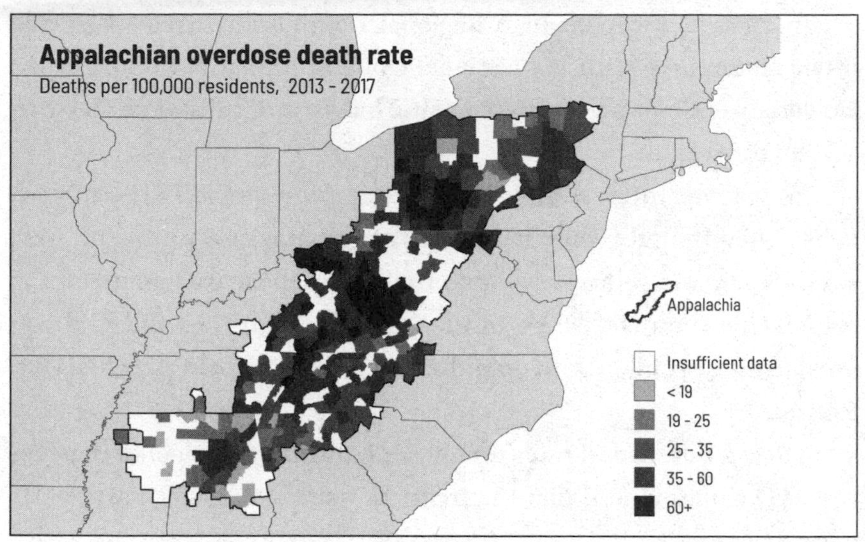

Now death rates are finally begin to crest—and in some cases even recede—in some of the hardest-hit areas.

But the risk of overdose is just one part of an addiction crisis that has metastasized to inflict harm on nearly every aspect of life in Appalachian communities. Addiction is tearing apart families and the social safety net. It is accelerating the spread of infectious disease, such as Allie's hepatitis C, and even reaching into a new, unborn generation, as with Mary's infant son.

The combined human toll of this suffering is incalculable, and the economic cost is hard to fathom. Researchers at the conservative American Enterprise Institute gave it a try, adding up the estimated costs of death and disease for each affected state.[4] West Virginia had by far the nation's highest costs per person; AEI pegged it at $4,378 per resident. There are about 1.8 million people in the state, so that math works out to roughly *$8 billion*. For one state.

Of course, we had plenty of warning about what was coming.

Michael Meit is a rural health researcher who spent a good part of his early career in the Appalachian reaches of Pennsylvania, where he became familiar with the growing addiction problem.

In 2008, the Appalachian Regional Commission asked Meit and other researchers with the National Opinion Research Center, at the University of Chicago, to assess mental health and substance abuse issues in the region.

"What was interesting is that they commissioned that study because they thought they had a methamphetamine problem," Meit said. He and his colleagues found that meth abuse was no greater in Appalachia than elsewhere in the country. What they did find was an alarming problem with opioid abuse, primarily pain pills like OxyContin.

Their report found rates for abuse "higher in Appalachia than the rest of the nation" and that the trend "is rising at a faster pace in Appalachia."[5]

The report linked the areas with the greatest increasing rates of opioid addiction to the places with the greatest levels of economic distress. And many of those were the coal mining and coal-dependent counties.

"Coal mining areas within the Appalachian region demonstrate higher rates of both heroin use and other opiates," the researchers wrote, and the "pace of these rate increases is even faster in coal mining areas than in other areas within the Appalachian region."

Meit and his colleagues had spotted the early flares of a crisis. They pulled the alarm, but the fire raged on.

"And again, that was in 2008," Meit said. "So it's been kind of a stark contrast to me that it's taken another ten, eleven years for people to really understand the nature of the crisis."

In 2017, Meit and his colleagues at the University of Chicago's Walsh Center for Rural Health Analysis revisited the topic of opioid addiction for the ARC. This time their report carried a grim, evocative title: "Appalachian Diseases of Despair."[6] These include deaths from alcohol and alcoholic liver disease, suicide, and, especially, overdose from prescription and illicit drugs.

Appalachia has long experienced significant disparities in health outcomes compared to the rest of the country, with rates of cancer, obesity, diabetes, and heart disease higher than the national averages. In 1999, the mortality rate for Appalachians was about 12 percent higher than the national rate. But the Walsh Center report found that the gap is widening, largely due to diseases of despair.

From 1999 to 2014, the United States as a whole enjoyed progress in health outcomes, and mortality among people aged fifteen to sixty-four steadily declined by about 10 percent. In Appalachia, however, mortality for that age group *increased* by 5 percent. By 2015, the mortality rate in Appalachia was 32 percent higher than for the rest of the country. The gap between Appalachia and the country as a whole had nearly tripled over fifteen years.

"So across the Appalachian region, we saw that overdose mortality rates were 65 percent higher than the rest of the country, which is just astonishing," Meit said.

And, as with the earlier work, the researchers again found even greater disparities in the coal-producing regions with the greatest economic distress. In terms of overdose deaths, distressed counties had a mortality rate 34 percent higher than even neighboring Appalachian counties not in distress.

"The biggest challenge is in central Appalachia," Meit said.

In the area where Kentucky, Ohio, and the Virginias meet—the heart of Appalachian coal country—the mortality from diseases of despair was ninety-four deaths per one hundred thousand people. That's more than 80 percent higher than the rest of the United States.

Meit's team recently went back to examine more recent data and found another disturbing trend. In two years' time, suicide in Appalachia went from 20 percent higher than the rest of the nation to 30 percent higher than the rest of the nation.

"That's a fifty percent increase relative to the rest of the nation in just two years," he said. "So I think there's another crisis looming that's not yet getting attention."

THE APPALACHIAN EXPERIENCE with opioids is a window into a complex national crisis tangled in corporate greed, inequality, and despair amid a fraying social fabric. The epidemic grew from a massive influx of pain pills pumped into a poor region by pharmaceutical companies like Purdue Pharma, maker of OxyContin, and the distributors and pharmacy companies that shipped and sold OxyContin and other, similar drugs.

Reporter Eric Eyre at the *Charleston Gazette-Mail*, who would go on to win a Pulitzer Prize, worked to unseal court records in West Virginia that documented the flood of pain pills into the state's small towns. Some 780 million doses of hydrocodone and oxycodone flowed in over a five-year period, at the height of the state's crisis. That was more than four hundred pain pills for every man, woman, and child in the state.[7]

Pain pills paved the way for heroin, then fentanyl. Now the crisis is evolving with the rise of new, more potent drugs and eruptions of needle-borne diseases that threaten to explode into epidemics of their own. Yet amid all this, communities are taking action, changing attitudes about addiction, and crafting solutions that can serve as models for other parts of the country.

POWELL COUNTY, KENTUCKY

After years of steadily climbing death rates, public health officials in the region began pushing their states to expand what are called harm-reduction programs. These simple programs, often housed in public health clinics, provide access to disease testing, referrals for addiction treatment, supplies of overdose-reversal drugs, and, often, needle exchange services to encourage the use of clean syringes.

In the spring of 2015, that work took on much greater urgency. Austin, Indiana, a town of about four thousand people in the state's south, saw an outbreak of nearly two hundred HIV cases, largely stemming from needle drug use.

In response, legislators passed laws allowing health departments to create needle exchange programs by local ordinance. Then focus shifted to the county level, where needle exchange programs faced considerable resistance.

"There are a lot of assumptions about the clients who use our program, that they are violent, that they are dangerous," Lynnsey McGarrh said. She holds the title of needle exchanger at the Lexington-Fayette County Health Department, which was one of the first places in Kentucky to enact a needle exchange program. The successful program has countered those misconceptions and taken tens of thousands of dirty needles out of use. It's also where Allie got tested for hepatitis C.

But Lexington, home to a large research university and center of the state's horse-racing wealth, is far different from the poor, rural, and culturally conservative counties in the state's east. It was in Appalachian coal country, exactly where it was most needed, that state public health officials knew they faced the highest hurdles in establishing a needle exchange.

Powell County, in eastern Kentucky, would be an early test.

"I actually called several of my friends and told them, 'Pray that this will not happen here,'" Mandy Watson said. Watson is a nurse at the Powell County Board of Health. She couldn't imagine a needle exchange program in her hometown, Clay City.

Troy Brooks is a physician assistant at the Powell County Board of Health. Like Watson, Brooks was against needle exchanges. It seemed to him like a way to let addicts keep using drugs rather than facing the consequences of their behavior.

Watson and Brooks shared many of the concerns that people frequently have about needle exchanges: that they will encourage drug use and attract other users and dealers from around the region, bringing with them crime and the risk of disease.

Powell County lies where the rolling hills of Kentucky begin to turn steeper and more rugged. The Red River carves a beautiful gorge through the sandstone here, with sheer walls and natural bridges that have become a mecca for rock climbers and hikers from around the world.

But the county has struggled to translate that tourism traffic into enough steady employment and income to offset the losses in mining and other industries. All the while, the effects of the addiction crisis were spreading.

Brad Epperson grew up in Powell County. He had lived for a little more than ten years in Tennessee before returning to pastor the Clay City First Church of God. He hardly recognized the town. The impact of drug addiction was everywhere.

At the church, he conducted too many funerals for people far too young. Epperson is also a school bus driver, and he could see the pain in the lives of the kids he carries. One day, he recalled, a boy excitedly told him that both his parents were going to be out of jail at the same time for Christmas. No child, Epperson said, should have that kind of life.

Pastor Brad Epperson had to reconsider his own views about those in addiction before he could support a needle exchange program in his community. "I don't think we can stand by and say, 'Well, we're going to give up on them,'" he said.

Epperson, too, balked at the thought of a needle exchange program. He sees addiction as a disease with a moral underpinning. Addicts make the choice to take in that first drug, knowing it is a sin. And addicts do other sinful things that don't fit with what most people consider the effects of a disease. Cancer patients don't steal from Mammaw to pay for chemo. Diabetics don't infect their spouses. He struggled with how to help people without appearing to condone the sinful behavior of drug abuse.

But he knew he and his congregation had to do something. Sitting on top of the Bible on Epperson's desk was a list of goals for his church, written in a looping, cursive hand. Near the top, it read: "Our community ought to see the love of God in us, not just by our understanding of a compassionate Gospel, but our public acts of love."

WHEN RESEARCHERS at the Centers for Disease Control and Prevention looked for the places in the country most at risk for outbreaks of needle-borne diseases such as HIV and hepatitis C, they found them in the central Appalachian counties of Kentucky, Ohio, and West Virginia. The CDC's 2016 analysis found nearly a hundred counties in the three states at high risk.[8] The ten counties the CDC identified as highest risk in the country were all in the coalfields of eastern Kentucky and southern West Virginia.

Since that work was published, both Kentucky and West Virginia have reported clusters of HIV infections in towns with populations under fifty thousand. Kentucky leads the nation in hepatitis C infection rates. Hospitals in the region struggle to treat patients who need heart valve transplants due to endocarditis, another infection caused by needle drug use.

For the past few years, the region has also been fighting the nation's deadliest outbreak of hepatitis A in recent memory, with nearly five thousand cases and sixty deaths. Not long ago, hep A was on the decline in the United States, but the combination of homelessness and needle drug use has brought it roaring back.[9]

Powell County ranked fifteenth in the nation on the CDC's analysis of counties at greatest risk of needle-borne disease outbreaks. Wolfe County, just next door, topped that list.

In Powell County's Clay City, Pastor Epperson learned some of these stats about health risks in a presentation about the proposed needle exchange program, a proposal he had been against. He thought deeply about his position and what his church owed to those in addiction.

"They are made in the image of God. They're highly redeemable. I believe that with all my heart," Epperson said in his pastor's study. "I don't think we can stand by and say, 'Well, we're going to give up on them.'"

Troy Brooks, the physician assistant, had a friend on the local police force whose job now included the regular collection of dirty needles from public places. He kept them in a plastic water bottle in his squad car to avoid an accidental stick.

"He went out to the Clay City playground, and I think he collected forty-one needles that had been stashed in different places around the playground," Brooks said. "That put me over the edge."

Mandy Watson, the nurse, also saw a presentation about the potential effects of an HIV outbreak in her town. She listened to the statistics about how infection rates could be lessened. She thought to herself, even if she couldn't cure the addict, she could help someone to be just a little bit safer and limit the risks.

"We are all very close. We all know each other here," she said, "and the thought of knowing that hep C and HIV outbreaks could happen very easily here, it scared me."

She changed her prayer request to friends. Now she asked that they pray *for* the needle exchange program.

In small communities like Powell County, there are no six degrees of separation. Often, it's just one or two. Epperson, Watson, and Brooks all went to school together. And once they changed their minds to work for the needle exchange program, they formed a powerful trio of trusted local voices.

They also found support from another Powell County native, Kevin Hall, who is spokesman for the Fayette County Health Department in Lexington. Hall provided a template based on how the Fayette County program works and helped make presentations to Powell County officials. And, as it turns out, Hall and Brooks are brothers-in-law.

In the fall of 2016, the Powell County Fiscal Court, the Board of Health, and a local city council all unanimously approved the creation of a needle exchange program. It was among the first in rural, conservative eastern Kentucky and the beginning of a trend. By the fall of 2019, there were sixty-three syringe programs in fifty-six Kentucky counties, including Wolfe County, which the CDC had identified as the highest risk in the nation.[10]

The communities are at the forefront of a shift in how addiction is perceived, toward viewing drug abuse as an illness rather than a crime, rethinking the use of stigmatizing terms such as "addicts," and reframing the problem as a public health challenge.

THAT PARADIGM SHIFT is also evident in the facilities now operating throughout Appalachia to help pregnant women in the throes of addiction and their children who are just coming into this world already harmed by opioids.

Again, central Appalachia is seeing the highest incidence of this. In West Virginia, with the nation's highest rate of babies born affected by drugs, a little more than 5 percent of all babies born in the state in 2017 were diagnosed with NAS. Health records show that in Kentucky, Ohio, and West Virginia combined, 14,881 babies born between 2013 and 2016 were affected by drugs they were exposed to in the womb.[11]

Many of those children are now approaching school age, and educators around the region report a sharp increase in the number of young children exhibiting behavioral and learning problems.

Tom Gibbs, the superintendent of the Athens City School District in southeastern Ohio, was watching students file downhill from an Athens elementary school to waiting buses and parents' cars, a daily

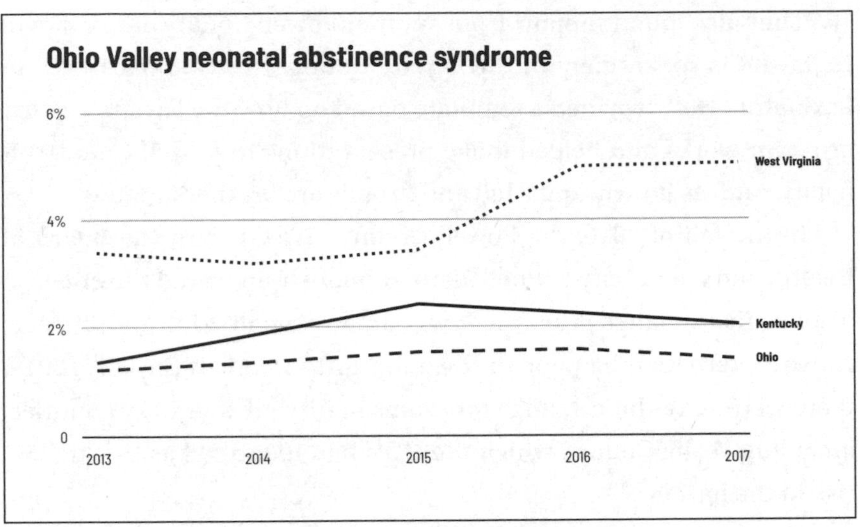

ritual to ensure the nearly three thousand students he watches over make it home safely.

Gibbs has been in education for three decades, and in recent years he's noticed a change: more young students with cognitive and emotional issues.

"Where we used to have one child each preschool group" with such issues, Gibbs said, "we now might have three to six." That's also true for kindergartners, he said, and teachers are puzzled and concerned.

"Our teachers are put in situations where they have to try to react to symptoms without knowing what the root causes of the challenges are," he said.

At nearby Ohio University, Sue Meeks, a registered nurse, was noticing a similar uptick in symptoms among three- and four-year-olds in the family navigator program she manages.

"Children who appear to be neurologically very overstimulated," she said, "often aren't social in your typical way. They don't respond to trying to calm them or trying to divert their attention to something else, laughing with them, or getting a response from reading."

She saw delays in language and motor development. The symptoms did not line up with the typical presentation of autism or ADHD for children of that age. But there was a common denominator: exposure to drugs in the womb.

Advancements in treatment have helped relieve withdrawal symptoms for both mother and baby. Now researchers are turning attention to the potential long-term effects. Researchers especially want to better understand how NAS affects the ability to learn so that parents, schools, and communities are prepared to help these children reach their developmental milestones.

"It's a multipronged mystery that I'm not sure that we will ever totally solve," Meeks said.

Dr. Henrietta Bada is a professor of pediatrics at the University of Kentucky and a prominent voice in NAS research. She said it can be difficult to tell what is caused by NAS and what is due to other factors associated with addiction. A delay in verbal communication, for example, could be caused by trauma experienced at home rather than NAS.

"The environments that these kids grow up in are not the best environments," Bada said. "That's when you try to balance the risk of a poor environment and then what happened to these kids when they were exposed to substances."

One study on learning and long-term effects of NAS came from Australia in 2017, where researchers compared the academic progress of students who had a history of prenatal drug exposure with a group of students with similar demographics but not born with NAS.[12]

The mean test scores of the children born drug-affected were lower than those of their counterparts. The results worsened as the students aged into high school.

Researchers in Tennessee more recently released a study of children enrolled in the state's Medicaid program. They found that one in seven children with a history of opioid exposure in the womb required services for developmental delays.[13]

While research continues, Bada said it is important to avoid stigmatizing affected children. "Let's not repeat what happened during the cocaine epidemic," Bada said.

In November 2017, Bada presented some of her work to a gathering of researchers from colleges and universities from around the region. It was the first meeting of the Ohio River Valley Addiction Research Consortium, organized by Northern Kentucky University.

The keynote speaker was journalist Sam Quinones, whose book *Dreamland* linked the economic malaise of the region and the greed of pharmaceutical companies to the origin of the opioid epidemic.

Now Quinones was pitching a potential solution, one he saw starting to take root with the people in that conference room. The place where the epidemic hit first and hardest, he said, could be the cutting edge of a cure as a regional research hub on addiction.

He pointed to a historical precedent not far away. A federal prison and hospital known as the Narcotics Farm, near Lexington, Kentucky, was a national center for addiction treatment and studies for decades, beginning in the 1930s. Clients included jazz greats Sonny Rollins and Chet Baker, actor Peter Lorre, and William S. Burroughs, whose novel *Junky* includes his "Lexington Visit."

The "narco farm," as it was known locally, helped develop the use of methadone as a treatment for withdrawal and did important research on drugs with the potential to block the brain chemistry behind opioids. The addiction work ended in the 1970s, when the facility was converted to a prison.

Quinones was calling for a new regionwide, collaborative approach to solving the opioid crisis. "I believe this region, southern Ohio, West Virginia, eastern Kentucky, can be a worldwide center for causes and treatment of addiction," he said, urging a holistic approach that considered work, faith, education, and community.

"The antidote to heroin isn't naloxone," he wrote later. "It's community."

Something like what Quinones described is beginning to take shape. The Ohio River Valley Addiction Research Consortium has continued its collaborative work on NAS, and other institutions in the region have launched ambitious, broad-based efforts on addiction research and treatment.

In 2019, the University of Kentucky received its largest grant in school history, $87 million, for a four-year program to reduce opioid overdose.[14]

Huntington, West Virginia, a town of about forty-eight thousand, made headlines a few years ago for a mass overdose event—more than twenty-six emergency overdose responses in just four hours. Now Huntington bills itself as a city of solutions, with rapid-response teams for people who survive overdoses and drug treatment for inmates at the local jail.

Marshall University in Huntington works with the local homeless shelter on Project Hope for Women and Children, a residential facility where mothers struggling with addiction can live with their children as they get help.

Huntington is also home to Lily's Place, a shelter for mothers in recovery. Lily's Place has been recognized for pioneering best practices for mothers and children with NAS and inspired federal legislation that makes it easier for other communities to set up similar facilities.

Karen's Place in Louisa, Kentucky, opened in early 2017. The facility is in a refurbished home in a secluded area, with staff support and amenities for both mother and baby around the clock.

"We're not going to have true compassion for the babies until we have true compassion for the moms," CEO Tim Robinson said.

Babies stay amid low lights and low noise to avoid overstimulation. Mothers get a balance of medically assisted addiction treatment, counseling, and a faith-based element for those who draw strength from their religious belief.

One of the first women to live in Karen's Place was Mary, the mother of two we met earlier in the chapter. Mary was determined to give her second baby a healthy start. She reached sobriety a few months into her pregnancy, and her second child was born with no signs of being affected by opioids. "It's been amazing," she said. "He's healthy, happy. He's a calm little guy."

Living at the maternity center has allowed Mary to focus on her continued recovery, motherhood, and her faith. She hopes to continue her education and someday help other mothers suffering with addiction.

"I've always encouraged people," she said. "If they're still breathing, there's still hope."

PROFILE:

The Doctors Facing the Crisis

One is a daughter of Appalachia's coal country. The other is the son of South Asian immigrants. But both Dr. Patrice Harris and Dr. Rahul Gupta, two of the leaders in the fight against opioids, were inspired by the crisis unfolding in the place they call home.

Gupta was born in India and spent much of his childhood in the suburbs of Washington, DC. He returned to India for medical training at the University of Delhi. Then came peripatetic years of work and study, including a residency at Northwestern in Chicago, a master's in public health in Alabama, and an MBA in London.[1]

Gupta made his way to West Virginia in 2009 to direct the health department serving Kanawha County and Charleston, the state capital. By that time, the state was already ground zero for the opioid epidemic.

"When I hear parents say, 'I'd rather have my child arrested and put in prison because that way I know that person will be alive,' that's the most heart-wrenching part of this," Gupta said.

Six years later, when he was appointed chief health officer for the state, the epidemic was a full-on emergency. The state had the nation's highest rates of addiction and overdose fatalities.

"Not a day goes by that I'm not constantly thinking about it," Gupta said. “We’re losing three, three and a half West Virginians per day. So the clock’s always ticking in my head.”

In 2016, 830 residents fatally overdosed—in a state with just about 1.8 million people. Gupta set about trying to understand what was driving that grim statistic. He found the medical literature useful when it came to the more obvious risk factors, but it wasn’t helping him understand the epidemiology of the disease.

“Rather than just continue to count numbers, let’s start to understand those lives that have been lost,” Gupta said. “We wanted to see who these individuals were.”

In partnership with state health researchers, he compiled detailed data about each overdose death for a process he called a “social autopsy.” From that data, the team created a profile of what a person at high risk of overdose was like and what sort of life he or she had been leading in the weeks and months before death. The study produced some surprising results.[2]

“We found that four out of five people who died in 2016 because of a drug overdose actually interacted with at least one of the health systems,” he said. “That means, for us, a unique opportunity to actually take advantage and prevent the overdose in the future.” They also found a high number of interactions with the criminal justice system and a high vulnerability to overdose just after incarceration—another opportunity for lifesaving interventions.

The approach was the first of its kind. The next step was putting the data to use.

“When primary providers, behavioral health providers, and others are seeing patients at clinics, we can show them these risk factors for overdosing and dying,” Gupta said.

It has taken years for the work to pay off, and the challenge has been intensified by the swiftly changing nature of the crisis and the arrival of new, more potent synthetic opioids. But statistics finally show overdose deaths beginning to level off. Gupta’s work has the potential to help other communities far beyond West Virginia as well.

Like Gupta, Dr. Patrice Harris draws upon her West Virginia experiences to drive the conversation about solutions.

"I was born and raised in Bluefield, West Virginia, in the heart of coal country," Harris said. "My father worked on the railroad. My mother taught school."

She earned her undergraduate degree in psychology, a master's degree in counseling psychology, and her medical degree from West Virginia University. She now practices psychiatry in Atlanta, but she keeps her connection to the mountains with regular home visits and by serving on the WVU Foundation board.

She began serving on the American Medical Association's board of trustees in 2011 and was nominated to serve as that board's chair from 2016 to 2017. In 2018, she was elected president of the AMA, the largest professional association for physicians in the United States. She is the first African-American woman to lead the AMA in its 171-year history.[3]

"I know that I can stand as tangible evidence that young girls from communities of color can aspire not only to be physicians but to be elected to the highest office of the physicians of this country," she said.

One of her major contributions has been leading the organization's opioid task force since its inception in 2011. The task force pushes for improvements in treating substance use disorder and for changes in the way many people—including physicians—think about the disease.

"We want to make sure we increase understanding that substance use disorder is a brain disorder," she said. "It's a chronic illness, just like diabetes and hypertension."

By the time Harris was leading the opioids task force, physicians were engaged in some deep soul-searching about their role in the origins of the crisis. So-called pill mills operated by unethical doctors dotted Appalachian towns for years, fueling widespread addiction. Even many well-meaning physicians sometimes overprescribed opioid pain pills thanks to false assurances from pharmaceutical companies about a low risk of addiction.

Harris is hoping to focus on what's working and change harmful practices.

"We highlight the decreasing number of opioid prescriptions that are written, around twenty-eight percent less nationwide over the last four to five years," she said. Physicians have also been enhancing education on pain treatment, she said, "so there is progress."

Still, there's a long way to go before physicians have the tools to properly make a dent in the addiction crisis.

"Across this country, only two in ten people who want opioid-use disorder treatment have access to it," she said. She wants to help expand access through support of the Affordable Care Act and by holding insurers accountable for parity. In some states, coverage for substance use disorders is not the same as coverage for other illnesses. She hopes to tackle that and other dysfunctional regulatory burdens to treatment.

"I may have to fill out a piece of paper or make several phone calls before a patient can get into treatment. Well, that delay in care could mean death," she said.

Though Harris's yearlong term as president had her traveling around the country, her ties to West Virginia still play a role in her work, giving her a deeper understanding of issues around access to health care. "I have a unique and personal connection and understanding of the region," she said, "and I'm back often."

In 2018, Rahul Gupta left West Virginia to become the chief medical and health officer for the March of Dimes. He plans to help the organization focus on mothers with opioid-use disorder and their babies born affected by the drugs in the mothers' bodies. That condition, neonatal abstinence syndrome, was a major problem he dealt with during his time in West Virginia.

He said his experience there has shaped his thinking, not just because of the region's problems but because of the people there: "people who are the most resilient, that spring back and fight for the right reasons and, at the end of the day, are able to find solutions when we feel that there aren't any."

8.
Growing a Recovery

IN THE ONCE-BUSY steel town of Wheeling, West Virginia, Doug Flight positions himself in front of a camera crew that's set up in his shop, Winkin' Sun Hemp Company.[1]

Flight has put in years learning how to grow and sell hemp, but apparently not so much time into memorizing his lines for this commercial.

"I know, I grow," Flight says to the camera. "Is that it?" Flight then asks a crew member.

"It's 'I know *because* I grow,'" someone with the camera crew answers back.

Take two.

Flight has wanted to shoot a regional television commercial for his hemp business since 2014, when he was among the first people in West Virginia's pilot hemp program. But local television stations turned him down. Hemp was then still illegal under federal law, lumped in with its infamous cannabis cousin, marijuana.

To farmers who knew hemp's history as a valuable crop for fiber, fabrics, oils, and seed, the ban was silly. Tetrahydrocannabinol, the psychoactive ingredient THC, was at levels so low in the plant that you'd need a hemp joint the size of a telephone pole to get high.

Luckily, reason prevailed with the Agricultural Improvement Act of 2018 (commonly known as the Farm Bill), which removed hemp from the list of controlled substances, redefining it as a legal crop. That will ease large-scale production and make growers eligible for research grants and crop insurance through the US Department of Agriculture. For a region in need of both jobs and a new cash crop, it's a no-brainer.

For Flight, the federal legalization of hemp meant television ads, banking opportunities, and much more. "It's going to allow me to get the message out about agricultural and industrial hemp, the products you can make from it," Flight said.

Flight's real bread and butter is CBD products. Cannabidiol oil is concentrated in hemp flowers, and its alleged benefits for anxiety, inflammation, and other ailments have been getting lots of press lately. The science behind those claims is still pretty thin, but that hasn't stopped the market from booming.[2]

And already farmers are fretting over just who will reap the real benefits. With some major corporate processors and marketers already circling, hemp could well follow in the footsteps of tobacco, where only a few made real money off the labor of many others. But there's hope that this newly rediscovered crop presents a chance to grow a new kind of agricultural model as well.

TONY SILVERNAIL swings a heavy machete at a stalk of bushy hemp and chops the plant near the root, grabbing the five-foot-tall shoot with his sun-weathered hand.

It's an unusually hot October day on his farm, Beyond the Bridge, tucked in the hills outside of Frankfort, Kentucky. But the heat doesn't faze Silvernail, who sports a sweat-soaked shirt, a huge smile, and a fat cigar between his teeth.

"Oh, I'm happy as hell," he said with a laugh.

Silvernail and hundreds of other farmers across the region were finally getting to harvest thousands of acres of hemp, the first full harvest since the law changed.[3]

Kentucky farmer Tony Silvernail harvests his first crop of hemp since it was legalized by the new Farm Bill. He helped to create an organic hemp cooperative for smaller hemp growers to take advantage of the new crop.

"This is actually the glory of being a farmer, as anybody whose livelihood depends on this can tell you. When you're harvesting, it's a happy time."

He's been an organic farmer for decades in Kentucky, but it wasn't until last fall when he and his business partner, Shawn Lucas, a professor at Kentucky State University, decided to try their luck at growing organic hemp for CBD production. Silvernail said when he first became an organic farmer in the 1990s, he appreciated the advice experienced farmers shared with newcomers in thc industry. But that hasn't been the case with hemp.

"I've really adopted that sense of helping, and you didn't really get that with the hemp industry. The hemp industry is still very closed," he said. "So I got in a bad mood." Silvernail was warming up to his story now. "Sitting there eating lunch with Shawn downtown, and I really came into a moment of 'You know, we just got to do our own thing.'"

The two set up an organic hemp cooperative for smaller hemp farmers. The cooperative purchases hemp seed and other supplies in bulk to get a better deal. It sells the members' collective hemp harvest to processors, using its strength in numbers to bargain for better prices. And the cooperative helps farmers figure out some basics of growing the crop in the first place.

Their cooperative is starting out small—fifteen farmers in central Kentucky growing about thirty acres—and has already seen some challenges. They unknowingly purchased faulty seed, and they've had thieves steal the crop right out of the fields. But Silvernail said it's all part of the learning process, even as he admits first-year sales numbers might be rough. "We can cry on each other's shoulders over a beer when we realize how badly we may have screwed up or what we didn't do, but hopefully next year will be better."

(Silvernail and other farmers got a hard lesson in just how volatile the emerging market can be. By early 2020, the rush to grow hemp had created a glut of supply; prices plunged, and a major hemp processor in Kentucky filed for bankruptcy.)

Cooperatives aren't a new idea in farming, but they're new in the hemp industry. Many small growers are choosing cooperatives to give themselves a better shot in an increasingly competitive marketplace.

Nathan Hall also sees hemp as a potential way to revitalize Appalachia's economy. He started the CBD hemp company Pine Mountain Remedies deep in rural eastern Kentucky.

Hall is from a family with deep roots in the Appalachian coalfields of Floyd County, Kentucky. Very early on, he said, he had his mind set on sustainable agriculture, but he knew he needed money to make it happen. Just out of high school, he went underground to work in a coal mine.

That didn't sit well with his grandparents. "They were worried

I was going to get killed in the mines," he said, and they convinced him to enroll at nearby Berea College. There he created an independent major in sustainable agricultural and industrial management. He later earned a joint master's degree in business and environmental management at Yale.

But Appalachia was never far from his mind, even when he was up north. Hall worked with some grant-supported programs that tried growing a range of crops on old surface mines in West Virginia, but the work needed to improve the damaged soil made the farming too costly.

While farming has always been part of central Appalachia's economy, it's rarely at the scale that much modern agriculture demands. The terrain is hilly and often rocky, and many rural communities are distant from major markets, making perishable produce impractical.

But hemp has promise.

"It's really one of the only things that I've noticed in my many, many years of now looking for feasible options for this area that meet all my criteria," he said. That is, it will not harm the land, has entrepreneurial opportunity, can employ enough people to make a difference, and has few health hazards.

"Other than the fact that you can throw your back out, you know, just moving stuff around," he said. The work is labor-intensive. The hilly terrain means that most of the small plots are on slopes or in "a crease" of a small drainage, making it hard to use large equipment. Hemp grown for CBD requires a light touch to protect the flowers, so much of the work is done by hand.

Hall says profit is not his first priority. He's more concerned with making sure the money made from hemp stays in the eastern Kentucky communities that have lost so many coal jobs. He's tired of state officials' repeated promises of economic development, which always seem to fall through.

"We have these proposed businesses that are going to build a thing on a former strip mine and it's going to create two hundred jobs, and it just never happens," Hall said.

He thinks hemp has sufficient value and durability to fit well with the available land and the distance to markets. His company combines leasing, revenue sharing, and sweat equity to give local people of different means the ability to participate in hopes of creating a stronger community through farming.

"I think it makes sense for this place," he said. "If you're willing to put in hard work and make good decisions, very timely decisions, you can actually have a decent income just on an acre or so of land back in the hills of Appalachia."

ALL OF THIS NEW agricultural energy in Appalachia has a strong echo of the past about it. Up through World War II, the region was among the country's top hemp producers. In fact, rope and other hemp-made materials helped win that war before hemp was banned as part of the same set of laws targeting marijuana.

But hemp never really went away. Anyone who grew up in the region can tell you that "ditch weed" remained a common sight along country roads where the plant continued self-seeding long after prohibition, as if waiting for its new moment.

On a deeper level, the hemp farmer-entrepreneurs today are drawing on Appalachia's historical roots, the thing that sustained mountaineers long before the big timber cuts, coal mines, and railroads that transformed the region.

"The people of the mountains have always loved to have their hands and their feet in the soil," Steven Stoll said. Stoll is a historian at Fordham University whose book *Ramp Hollow* tells the story of Appalachia's unique brand of agriculture and how it has largely been lost.

Stoll says Appalachian agriculture was primarily subsistence-level farming that depended heavily on the use of the commons. The commons might be the ridgetop pastureland that several families shared or the woods where they would hunt, gather firewood in fall, and, in the spring, harvest the ramps, or wild leeks, that give his book its title.

"It's a thriving, functioning ecology that produces a subsidy to the farm itself," Stoll explained. Without the commons, Appalachian life of that period would simply not have been possible.

But those early farmers and their commons sat atop billions of dollars' worth of coal. "And all they were doing was using it for cooking," Stoll said.

The arrival of mining companies set up a struggle for land that dispossessed some landowners and deprived others of the commons they needed to survive. Settlers were suddenly in a new world of capitalist commoditization with little to sell other than their labor. Many went to work in the coal mines. And that, in a nutshell, "is the story of where Appalachia comes from," Stoll said.

Now the story is where Appalachia goes from here. The return to farming shows that, much like ditch weed, the agricultural impulse never died. It just lay dormant.

"What we're basically saying is that coal, and this extractive industry, is not the end of the story," Stoll said. "If we're smart about it, it can be a new beginning of something different."

JONATHAN WEBB'S COMPANY AppHarvest is building what he calls one of America's biggest greenhouses on a plot of land near Morehead, not far from Interstate 64 in eastern Kentucky. The first of the planned greenhouses under construction now will cover sixty acres, or about the size of sixty football fields. A nearby retention pond will hold rainwater collected from the massive roof, supporting a hydroponic growing system for tomatoes and other produce.

Webb grew up in Kentucky, and said he wanted to do something that can help diversify the economy. "It's very frustrating to see how much of this region has, frankly, been left behind," he said. "Now is the time to reimagine, reinvest, and rebuild here."

But he also has a strong business argument for choosing the region.

"This isn't just a passion project. It's a really strategic location for us," he said. From I-64, his produce can get to 70 percent of the country within a day's drive, reducing transportation costs and making his tomatoes more competitive.

The Dutch have long been leaders in this sort of indoor growing, and Webb developed an exchange with experts in the Netherlands, even hosting trips for local officials. He's also proud of partnerships he's made with local schools to create what he calls an "ecosystem of high-tech ag."

"Before we've sold our first vegetable, we've made a nearly $150,000 investment in technology at Shelby Valley High School," he said. "We're giving young students the opportunity to figure out what farming in the future will look like."

Much of the money for all this is coming from venture capital, including the Rise of the Rest Seed Fund, which is part of the Revolution capital fund started by America Online founder Steve Case. Case worked with J. D. Vance, author of *Hillbilly Elegy*, and Vance was managing partner for the project, which counts Jeff Bezos of Amazon and former Google executive Eric Schmidt among its investors.[4]

Vance said "the rest" in the name refers to anyone outside the Silicon Valley, Boston, and New York tech centers, the places that take up about three-quarters of venture capital investment.[5]

"To us 'the rest' is pretty much everybody that's struggling over that small pot of money" that's left over, Vance said. "If only three states are getting most of the venture capital, that means only three states are getting most of the net job growth."

Vance and Case invite investors on bus tours of the Midwest, the South, and other overlooked parts of the country, hearing from entrepreneurs like Webb. AppHarvest was one of the fund's early investments.

Because of regional backlash against Vance's book, however, the money comes with a bit of baggage. His memoir of growing up amid addiction and abuse in Middletown, Ohio (not, by the way, in Appalachia), was a bestseller, and is soon to become a film directed by Ron Howard.

Vance's critics suggest his libertarian ideology led him to place too much emphasis on personal responsibility and blame the poor in Appalachia for their own predicament.

"*Elegy* is little more than a list of myths about welfare queens repackaged as a primer on the white working class," Sarah Jones wrote in the *New Republic* in one typically scathing review.[6] Jones (who grew up in Washington County, Virginia—an Appalachian county) argued that Vance's focus on personal choice and what she called the "imagined cultural failings of Appalachians" ignores the region's larger economic problems, which limit people's options in the first place.

The Vance backlash has started to spill over onto the AppHarvest brand, with some other farmers in the region taking to social media to complain that they'll soon be competing against J. D.'s venture capital tomatoes.

Others are simply skeptical of a venture capital approach to funding agriculture.

"This is a place where investors have shown up time and again, took their rate of return on capital, and left behind a mess," said Dee Davis, founder of the Center for Rural Strategies in Whitesburg, Kentucky. He compares venture capitalists, with the high rate of return they often seek, to the very extractive industries that Webb and other farmers are now trying to replace.

Davis expressed doubts about whether the venture capital model fits with the culture and the long-term planning for a recovery after coal's collapse.

"We'd love to have some thoughtful investment, some patient investment from people who understand what is really valuable here," Davis said. "If you can find investors who appreciate who we are, then bring 'em in."

Webb argues that his project does, in fact, represent that sort of patient investment. They've already overcome some setbacks. The first location for a greenhouse was to be on some old surface mine land that local officials were eager to put to productive use. (What better way to demonstrate the turn from old fossil fuels to new sustainable agriculture?) But putting such scarred land to new use is seldom easy. In this case, the uneven settling of the rock and dirt fill the mining company left behind made it unsuitable for the greenhouse construction.

All in all, Webb said he's optimistic. "A place that was formerly known for powering the country," he said, "is going to be known for growing healthy fresh fruits and vegetables."

Autumn McCraw is lead barista and helps with the desserts at Café Appalachia, where most of the workers are in recovery from addiction. "I have a whole support system here that understands," she said.

THERE ARE EVEN SIGNS that agriculture holds promise to help mend communities ravaged by the addiction crisis.

It's lunch hour, and Café Appalachia is bustling.

Located in South Charleston, West Virginia, the former church turned restaurant has a funky yet calming vibe. Twinkle lights and mismatched dining room sets dot the space. For $8 to $10 a plate, diners can enjoy a locally sourced meal like today's options of apple sage pork tips, spiralized zucchini (or "zoodles"), roasted broccoli, and a salad of spinach grown just a few miles away.

Autumn McCraw helped prepare today's meal. The thirty-five-year-old Charleston resident sports a maroon apron and greets every customer with a smile. Her days here typically start around 8:00 a.m.

"I start my tasks as the barista here, making coffee, making sure the tea's prepared. I also try my best to make the desserts," she says. "It's something that I really like to do."

But this café is more than just a job. It's a second chance. McCraw heard about Café Appalachia while participating in long-term addiction recovery treatment.[7]

"As addicts in society, we're shunned," she says. "To know that the community is supporting me and having my back is such an essential part of my recovery."

Almost everyone who works at Café Appalachia is in recovery, and McCraw says being part of a team that understands what that means and can support her has been a game-changer.

"If I'm struggling, if it happens to be one of those days, you know, I have a whole support system here that understands," she said.

Café Appalachia is one of many regional projects that put people in recovery in food service and agriculture jobs. Amid a crippling opioid crisis and crumbling economic base, Appalachians are looking to food systems as a way forward.

The café is part of a larger program called the Appalachian Food Enterprise, which got a federal grant to start both the café and an urban farm located just a few miles away, where Reggie Jones greets visitors.

"Welcome to Paradise Farms," Jones says as he walks guests into a greenhouse where ventilation fans whir above beds of greens. Jones is CEO of the Kanawha Institute for Social Research and Action, a project partner that's part of an integrated suite of farm-to-fork operations that blend business with social services.

"We want to be able to take a seed, put it in the ground, grow it, harvest it, process it, and get it out to the social enterprises, like the café, like the catering business, like the food truck, and create training opportunities and jobs along that entire continuum," Jones said.

A group of women in recovery begin their training at Paradise Farms, learning about farming and the food industry, both in the classroom and in the two hydroponic greenhouses. Then they can move to working at the café, food truck, and catering service. Jones said the project aims to create forty-two jobs for those in recovery, some just coming out of prison and others who need good experience to put on a résumé.

"Even if we don't ultimately hire them, they're still a marketable person because of the skills that they developed along that continuum."

Jones believes jobs in food and agriculture provide more flexibility for people in recovery, who might need to schedule appointments for things like therapy, than other service industries might.

Cheryl Laws is CEO and founder of Pollen8, another project partner. She thinks these projects can help tackle a number of West Virginia's health challenges. "We have the highest rate for obesity, and we have the highest rate for overdoses," she said. "But what we're trying to do with the Appalachian Food Enterprise is take that negativity and show how to fix it."

The idea is taking root all around the region. Jeannie Harrison is founder of Gro Huntington, a nonprofit that runs an urban farm managed by recovery clients from local treatment centers. "You can't grow a pepper and have someone say, 'That's a waste,'" Harrison said with a laugh. "Because food is fundamental. And I think that it's one of those great uniting things about just being a human."

Her group sells produce at the local farmers market and supplies restaurants, getting nutritious, high-quality produce to a community that often doesn't have good food options.

"We called it a 'food desert farm stand,' because we were in the middle of a food desert. Which means if you were a neighbor to the Gro farm, you did not have access to fresh food if you didn't have a car," Harrison said.

She has plans for a fruit orchard and a composting program as well, but, as with many of these projects, she is constantly trying to graft together a working budget from grants and philanthropic donations. She hopes others will see the benefits of recovery through a foundation of food.

"Fresh local food and work for people who may not be able to find it as easily? Absolutely. That is a powerful, powerful way to create change."

9.

Politicoal 1: Justice Delayed

DONALD TRUMP HAS been a frequent visitor to West Virginia, both as a candidate in 2016 and now as president. He holds rallies and attends events in the state he won with nearly 68 percent of the vote in 2016. West Virginia's governor, Jim Justice, thinks he knows why.

"You have a president of the United States of America that truly has an attraction to West Virginia," Justice told radio station WAJR.[1] "And his attraction to West Virginia, contrary to anything you may think, is me. That's it. That's all there is to it. It's just me."

Trump and Justice do have a lot in common. Both men are tall, something Trump likes to point out during events with Justice, or "Big Jim," as he calls him.

"He's a big man. He's all man," Trump said at one such rally in Charleston. "He's six feet, eleven inches tall," Trump declared, adding a few inches to Justice's actual height of around six feet, seven inches.

"I won't talk about the weight. I don't know what the weight is," Trump went on as Justice shuffled from the stage. "I won't go there."

Both men also command large fortunes. Justice is reportedly West Virginia's wealthiest citizen, with an estimated net worth somewhere between $1.5 billion and $1.9 billion, mostly from his agriculture holdings and numerous coal businesses, which he inherited from his father.[2]

West Virginia governor Jim Justice, a billionaire coal baron, was elected despite his mining companies' failure to pay millions in taxes and overdue mine safety violation fines.

Both are strong supporters of the coal industry who advance proposals to reduce regulatory restrictions and taxes on mining and burning coal.

Justice also owns a hotel, the luxury Greenbrier resort in West Virginia. And both were political outsiders who had never held office before winning executive positions in 2016.

But there is one key difference. Justice was elected as a Democrat. In the late summer of 2017, that party difference would change. Before a rally in Huntington in early August, Trump hinted at "a very big announcement" coming that evening in West Virginia.

"Come on up, Jim," Trump said to Justice at the rally. "Look at this guy!"

Justice announced from the stage that he was switching parties.

"I'll tell you West Virginians, I can't help you any more being a Democrat governor," Justice said, not quite eight months into his term. "The Democrats walked away from me."

Trump praised the move, but other Republicans in West Virginia were caught by surprise. The state party had regularly attacked Justice for ethical problems and for being a "deadbeat" on taxes.[3]

That's another thing that Trump and Justice have in common: questions about how much they pay, or do not pay, in taxes.

Trump, of course, famously refused to release his tax returns as a candidate and has since waged sustained court battles as president to keep his records private. For Justice, the taxes in question stemmed from his activity in the state's key industry: coal.

After his father's death in 1993, Justice inherited Bluestone Industries Inc. and Bluestone Coal Corporation. Those companies spawned a number of other coal operations across the Appalachian portions of Alabama, Kentucky, Tennessee, Virginia, and West Virginia.

In the months leading up to the gubernatorial campaign, local reports indicated that the Justice companies were not keeping up with some property and mineral taxes.[4] These taxes are mostly levied at the county level, on the coal a company mines and the reserves it holds. In many of those rural counties, these taxes are the local government's major source of revenue.

In 2016, NPR, Ohio Valley ReSource, and its partners investigated, visiting county courthouses and sorting through tax records, liens, and payment agreements around the region. We found that, all combined, Justice-owned companies owed roughly $15 million in overdue taxes and unpaid mine safety fines.[5]

Then-candidate Justice said those debts would be paid.

"When it all really boils right down to it, we're taking care of them," Justice said at a campaign event. "We'll absolutely, y'know, take, make sure that every one of them is taken care of."

One of Justice's lawyers, Billy Shelton, responded to NPR in a written statement, saying "the Justice Companies are being responsible and following the agreed-upon payment plan," and to "imply anything beyond that is purely for political reasons and ignores the facts."[6]

However, it would be years before the Justice companies would fully repay most of the tax obligations, and it would take a lawsuit from the Department of Justice to get them to begin to address overdue mine safety fines.[7]

All across the region, the ReSource found examples of county executives facing huge budget shortfalls, forced to make painful cuts in local services largely due to the missing revenue from unpaid taxes.

Knott County, Kentucky, had already been hit hard by the coal industry's decline. By 2016, the county budget was half of what it had been just seven years before. Knott County was also owed more than $2.3 million by Kentucky Fuel Corporation, the largest of any county debts the Justice companies owed at the time.[8]

"Every dollar that somebody doesn't pay puts a huge burden on the county," Zach Weinberg said. At the time Weinberg was Knott County's judge-executive, the county's top elected official. He described Kentucky Fuel as a "repeat offender" and explained that the county had already won two lawsuits against Justice's company to force payment of back taxes.

In August 2018, Governor Justice, by then a Republican, gathered the press for an announcement: "I think we can put to bed once and for all this tax issue that's been looming around forever more." Justice said the companies, now operated by his son, had paid all tax obligations—in West Virginia, that is.[9]

But the governor did not disclose the nature of the agreement with the state or what he was doing about taxes owed to other state and county governments, such as Knott County. A few phone calls confirmed that the Justice companies still owed millions in rural parts of Kentucky, Tennessee, and Virginia.[10] By that time, Weinberg and other officials around the region were taking more serious action. "He has not paid any more," Weinberg confirmed. "I mean, it's ridiculous, it really is. We took him to court. We got a summary judgment."

The court put Kentucky Fuel's Knott County property into receivership so that the county could try to make good on lost revenue. However, officials couldn't find a buyer.

"We ended up having to let a couple of our deputies go," Sheriff Dale Richardson said. "We only had five full-time deputies, and we're down to three. That puts that much more burden on us, and it really puts us in a bad way."

Richardson said the situation is made more frustrating because of the repeated attempts to recover debts.

"It's not these people's first rodeo," Richardson said.

The ReSource heard similar stories from other counties and states where Justice family companies operated.

In Magoffin County, Kentucky, then assistant county attorney Travis Joseph said he had set up a number of payment plans with Kentucky Fuel to address overdue taxes. However, he said, the payments stopped.

In Scott County, Tennessee, county trustee Jimmy Byrd watched interest pile up on back taxes the Justice companies owed.

And in Tazewell County, Virginia, where county officials said a Justice company owed more than $800,000, mild-mannered treasurer David Larimer had finally had enough. "Playing hardball was the only option," Larimer said in his soft country lilt.

He described walking around the coal mine's gravel driveway on a snowy day, using Scotch Tape to attach seizure orders to every piece of equipment he saw. "Continuous miners, ventilation systems, computers in the office," Larimer said. "We put notice on there that it was a felony to move it."

Eventually, Larimer worked with the county sheriff to seize equipment at the mine and arrange the sale of two massive Caterpillar trucks. That raised enough money to cover all but about $150,000 of the debt at the time, he said.[11]

"What's really galling is that they won't stick to a payment plan," Larimer said. He said Justice companies' nonpayment was "a pattern of behavior," not a single event. In order to make up the missing revenue, which the county's schools, public safety, landfill, and other services depend upon, officials would need to increase real estate taxes on other landowners.

Back in Knott County, Judge-Executive Weinberg was looking at a deficit from the combined impact of Justice's delinquent taxes and Kentucky's changes to the mineral tax valuation. He was also facing an election in 2018 and a tough decision: either cut county services further or find some other way to make up for the missing coal revenue.

"Nobody likes taxes," he said. "But we didn't have a choice."

He opted to raise the tax rate on some insurance premiums in the county, a very unpopular move in a place with per capita income of about $18,000 a year and a poverty rate above 30 percent. Then he faced county voters.

"Well, I just ran and got beat," Weinberg said with a rueful chuckle. Someone had finally faced political consequences for the Justice companies' failure to pay taxes—and that someone was Weinberg.

In June 2019, the Justice companies finally agreed to a settlement covering millions of dollars in overdue taxes in four eastern Kentucky counties, including Knott.[12]

Randy Slone, assistant attorney for the county, said that even when the county does manage to recover the tax debts, it will be something of a Pyrrhic victory. The damage to school and public safety budgets has already been done.

"Problem is, when I eventually collect that money, it's late," Slone said. "That hurts the school system and the county. It's not the same as getting it on time."

Call it Justice delayed.

UNPAID MINE SAFETY violations were another chronic problem for the Justice companies. In 2014, an NPR investigation showed that Justice companies owed just under $2 million in delinquent federal mine safety penalties, which are levied by the Mine Safety and Health Administration, or MSHA.[13] Two years later, when Jim Justice was running for governor, a follow-up investigation showed that the companies' debt had climbed to $2.6 million.[14]

As with the unpaid taxes, Justice pledged that those debts would be paid in full.

But a ReSource analysis of MSHA data for 2018 showed that more than four years after that initial investigation, the Justice companies—now mainly controlled by the governor's children, James Justice III and Jillean Justice—had still not significantly paid down their debt.

Instead, as of the end of 2018, the Justice companies' mine safety violation debt had ballooned to $4.3 million, far and away the highest such debt of any coal company in the country.[15] (MSHA only reluctantly shared the public data about unpaid safety debts. NPR had to threaten legal action under the Freedom of Information Act in order to win release of the information.)

Former federal mine safety officials and industry experts said the continued disregard for paying mine safety fines shows a lack of respect for the regulatory system created under the Mine Safety and Health Act to keep miners safe.

"[Gov. Justice] and his family have simply chosen to disregard, flagrantly violate, continually violate and increasingly violate the rules of mine safety and the penalties of mine safety," said Davitt McAteer, a retired lawyer and former head of MSHA during the Clinton administration.

"The signal that that sends to the whole state, and in fact the region or the coal industry, is that this is a person who has utter disregard for the agencies, for the people who do enforcement, and for their employees," McAteer continued.

About a month after the ReSource and NPR published the results of the investigation, the US Department of Justice filed a civil lawsuit against twenty-three Justice coal companies, seeking more than $4.7 million in unpaid fines and fees for mine safety and health violations.[16]

Thomas Cullen, US attorney for the Western District of Virginia, said in a news release that the companies had incurred nearly 2,300 mine safety and health violations over the previous five years and had ignored multiple demands by MSHA, the Department of the Treasury, and the US Attorney's Office to pay the delinquent debts.

"This is unacceptable, and, as indicated by this suit, we will hold them accountable," Cullen stated.

Michael Carey, a lawyer who represented the Justice companies, said in an interview that the Justices had been actively negotiating with both the US Attorney's Office and MSHA.

"The Justice companies are frustrated that the US Attorney's office decided to go through with this litigation at this point because we've been negotiating with them to resolve this matter for several months now," he said.[17]

On April 1, 2020, the Justice companies finally agreed to pay up. US attorney Cullen announced a civil settlement to collect all mine safety debts—more than $5 million—owed by twenty-four Justice-owned coal companies operating in Alabama, Kentucky, Tennessee, Virginia, and West Virginia. The government counted 2,297 citations against the Justice entities for violations of the Mine Safety and Health Act between 2014 and 2019.[18]

The Justice companies often dispute state and federal regulators' claims that the companies lag behind in the required reclamation of damaged mine lands, arguing that they inherited problems from previous mine owners. Further, Governor Justice has frequently defended his family companies by pointing out that they could have filed for bankruptcy protection, as many coal companies have. By keeping the companies out of bankruptcy, he argued, they can repair mine lands when market conditions improve, and states and counties at least have the option of future tax revenue. It was a point he made in a debate back in 2016 during his run for governor.

"Jim Justice has never bankrupted any company," he said. "It would've been an easy way. Just shut the doors. Let everybody get stuck. I didn't do it. I promise you that every single obligation that I ever have will be fulfilled."

But the company makes frequent use of a sort of regulatory gray zone called “mine idling,” which is somewhere between operating a mine full-time and shutting it down for good. Those idled mines can create problems for the surrounding community even when the company has not gone bankrupt.

From an overlook on the top of Black Mountain—the highest point in Kentucky—the wooded Appalachian mountains stretch on like a wavy sea of green for miles into Wise County, Virginia, just across the state border.

Amid the lush forest, barren brown spots mar the landscape. These are the scars from surface coal mines, created when the sides or entire tops of mountains were scraped and blasted away to get to the coal seams below. One sprawling mine in particular, with its towering cliff walls, dominates the view.

“Looney Ridge Surface Mine No. 1,” Matt Hepler said. Hepler is an environmental scientist with the advocacy group Appalachian Voices,

The unreclaimed mine land on Looney Ridge, near the border between Kentucky and Virginia, is among the many idled mines owned by the Justice family. “When mines become inactive or idle, they starve a local community,” said Joe Pizarchik, former head of the US Department of the Interior’s Office of Surface Mining Reclamation and Enforcement.

and he has become very familiar with this view of the mine, which has remained an ugly blemish on the hills.

For years he has been following action, or lack thereof, at the Looney Ridge mine, which is operated by A&G Coal, a company run by the Justice family. Coal has not been produced here since at least 2013, when A&G Coal asked Virginia regulators to place the mine in what is called temporary cessation.[19] The permit status allows mining to pause, giving mining companies flexibility on requirements for land reclamation until it becomes more economically feasible to begin extracting coal again. As the name implies, this idling is supposed to be temporary—but it turns out "temporary" is a very flexible word.

A 2019 analysis of mine permit data conducted by the Center for Public Integrity found that central Appalachia is home to about half of all idled coal mines in the country, and many have been in that status for years.[20] The long-term idling of mines via this permit status can throw workers and nearby communities into limbo and delay crucial environmental cleanup.

The CPI analysis shows that of all the country's coal mining companies, the Justice companies make the most frequent use of idling. As of 2019, thirty-three mines and a coal preparation plant owned by the Justice family's companies were idled, and fifteen of them had been in that status for at least three years. In West Virginia, one Justice mine, in McDowell County, has been idled for almost a decade.

In Virginia, state mining regulators entered into a compliance agreement with the Justices in early 2014, in an attempt to force the Justice company to reclaim the Looney Ridge site. But five years later, Matt Hepler could still stand on Black Mountain and point to the same broken-down bulldozer that had been sitting on the damaged mine land for years.

"It's looked like this for as long as I've been coming up here," he said.

A spokesperson for the state said the agency is "doing everything within our enforcement authority" to push the Justices to clean up the site. A spokesperson for the Justice companies defended the reclamation work and said idling permits are standard practice across the industry. But idled mines, especially those left untouched for years at a time, can negatively affect the economy, health, and environment of nearby communities.

"When mines become inactive or idle, they starve a local community, and they deprive the community of the coal mining jobs and other related jobs," said Joe Pizarchik, head of the US Department of the Interior's Office of Surface Mining Reclamation and Enforcement during the Obama administration. OSMRE is the federal agency in charge of regulating surface coal mines.

"It's not making money on anything for anybody for the community, and it can be a potential pollution source," he said.

Emily Bernhardt is an ecosystem ecologist and biogeochemist at Duke University's Nicholas School of the Environment. Bernhardt explained that, in addition to being unsightly, there are health and safety risks associated with mines left unreclaimed for long periods.

Mines left idled can expose residents to coal and silica dust. They can also pose a risk for landslides and flooding. During surface coal mining, operators often pile tons of rock and liquid behind earthen dams. When left idle, she said, those impoundments face a greater likelihood of failing.

"You can't actually make any improvements when you're just sort of on hold," Bernhardt said.

Larry Bush is all too familiar with how those effects play out for the communities near an idled surface mine. Bush worked as both a coal miner and a mine inspector for years after his service in Vietnam. Now retired, he lives in the town of Appalachia, Virginia, not far from two Justice company mines—one that is active and the idled mine at Looney Ridge.

Bush sipped a sports drink while sitting under a gazebo at a park in town, wearing his customary veteran's ball cap and aviator glasses.

"There's a little stream that's pretty much filled up with silt," he said, describing the effects he sees from the strip-mining and erosion from the idled mine. "Nothing can live in it."

Bush would like this region to use its natural beauty to rebound with a tourism-based economy as the coal industry declines. But he struggles to see how that can happen with idled mines marring the landscape.

"If they're not actively employing people or actively working the site, they should be forced to actually do their reclamation work, instead of just leaving raped-out mountains," he said.

There is a logic behind the rules that allow a company to temporarily idle a mine. The fluctuating prices for coal and the boom-bust nature of the business can make it hard for companies to maintain consistent production and employment and thus afford to keep up with required reclamation. The idle status provides some flexibility to pause production in a down cycle until coal prices rebound.

That's the theory. But these days, the dominant industry trend in coal runs in just one direction: down.

Pizarchik, the former federal mine regulator, worries that the industry's decline further reduces the chances that idled mines will ever be addressed. "I believe it's extremely unlikely that those mines will ever be activated again, because the price of coal is never going to go up," he said. "The demand will only continue to shrink."

And if operators walk away from idled mines, it could leave taxpayers on the hook for reclamation.

In Virginia, for example, minutes from an April 2017 Coal Surface Mining Reclamation Fund Advisory Board meeting show that the Justice company mines alone have an estimated $200 million worth of cleanup liabilities.

Several mining states allow coal operators to "self-bond" for reclamation costs. That is, they put up a cash bond or buy a bond from an insurance firm if a company is deemed to be in good financial health. Virginia is moving away from that practice, because it can increase the risk that the bonding will not be sufficient to cover environmental costs. But according to state officials, some A&G Coal permits remain self-bonded—which means that if the company goes under, the state gets none of the money required for cleanup.

In the past, the state has allowed coal companies to pay only partial bond amounts into a shared pool. The bond pool is meant to supplement cleanup for more than 150 permits, but the pool currently has less than $10 million in cash.

In the case of A&G Coal, the reclamation would cost more than what's in the pool bond, said state spokeswoman Tarah Kesterson. "So that's why we're trying to work with them, to get them to pay for the reclamation."

UNRECLAIMED MINES are a common problem across coal country, and the Justice companies are hardly unique in an industry with chronic issues relating to erosion, runoff, and pollution from old mines. But even by those standards, the Justice companies stand out for a number of high-profile controversies involving epic legal disputes with regulators and repeated allegations of damage to the surrounding communities.

Well before Justice became governor, his companies had already racked up hundreds of violations and millions in fines in Kentucky for failing to restore land that they'd mined. The state negotiated multiple rounds of orders to complete the work, but officials found the companies were not complying, so the state took Justice to court for a series of lawsuits that took years to play out.[21]

Bevins Branch, a Justice company mine in eastern Kentucky's Pike County, is one of the mines in question.[22] The people living nearby say they are continually paying the price whenever heavy rains bring the company's mess downhill to their doorsteps.

On October 4, 2018, that rain started around 10:30 p.m. By midnight, the creek in front of Elvis and Laura Thacker's house had grown to a mighty flood, uprooting trees, moving boulders, and surging right up to the couple's front steps.[23] The Thackers decided to abandon their home, but when they got into their jeep, they found the flood had washed the road away, leaving them trapped.

"Water was everywhere," Laura Thacker remembered. The couple lay awake most of that night, afraid their whole house would be destroyed.

The hilly terrain of eastern Kentucky where the Thackers live is prone to flash flooding. But this was no normal flood, and it was not the first time they'd been hit. A similar incident damaged their home in 2016.

The Thackers live about a quarter mile downhill from Bevins Branch. The mine had been scheduled for reclamation by 2015, work that would include eliminating highwall rock cliffs, restoring the contours of hills, controlling water runoff, and planting vegetation to keep soil in place.

By that date, lawyers for the Justice companies were asking for an extension on the work deadline. A new completion date was set for March 2016.

In a report produced for that deadline, state officials said they had "not observed any measurable progress on highwall reclamation" at Bevins Branch.

More than two years later, Bevins Branch remained a point of contention between the Justice companies and the state, and reclamation remained unfinished. Kentucky's Energy and Environment Cabinet inspectors found the Justice family companies were at fault for contributing to multiple flooding incidents affecting households like the Thackers'.

In the 2018 incident the Energy and Environment Cabinet issued two violations. "Mining activities have adversely impacted the hydrologic balance," an inspector wrote. By allowing diversion ditches to fill up with sediment and debris, the mining company caused an "uncontrolled discharge" of water runoff.[24]

Richard Getty, a lawyer for the Justice companies, disputed the state's findings: "If there are problems because of the heavy rain and an act of God, that's beyond our control; that's not our responsibility." The Justice companies had made significant progress in addressing violations that had been inherited from the site's previous owners, Getty said. "I believe the Justice companies should be applauded for all of this continuous effort."

The Thackers said they'd been offered some money by Justice's company after the 2016 flooding event, but not enough to cover the losses. The damage came at an especially bad time, because they'd only recently achieved some financial stability after a rough patch. Elvis lost his coal job years earlier, they had lost a car and a truck, and for years they worked two jobs apiece, trying to stay afloat. Then they had to deal with the flood damage to the house.

The morning after the flood, huge rocks and great tongues of mud

Flood damage that state regulators attribute to runoff and mudslides from a surface coal mine owned by the Justice family in Kentucky. "You're really afraid to lay down and go to sleep at night," said eighty-one-year-old resident Betty Short.

were everywhere, covering yards and driveways. Elvis picked his way among the debris, stopping here and there to point out the labeled bailing material and other identifiable items that had washed down from the mine site. The Thackers were relieved when their dog came trotting up the damaged road. They had feared he was washed away in the night.

The community's main road was cut in half. The rushing water had ripped away the asphalt and left a deep crevice in place of a culvert. Several neighboring houses were affected.

Betty Short lives alone in a brown house not far from the Thackers, across the road from the mouth of the hollow. She's eighty-one years old. In the 2016 flood, thick mud covered every inch of her property, she said, and when she tried leaving the house she slipped in the muck, breaking her collarbone. Short said she got a lawyer but has seen no money for her injury.

In the second flood in 2018, Short was unharmed, and she didn't think her house had sustained damage. Already, she was making the best of the situation. "At least this time I know to stay out of the mud," she laughed.

Short was grateful that neighbors came to check on her. Life next to the mine brings a constant anxiety, made worse whenever the rains come. "You're really afraid to lay down and go to sleep at night," she said. "It's like a nightmare. You never know what's going to happen next."

10.
Politicoal 2: Trump Country Revisited

FOR THOSE WHO follow the business and politics of coal in West Virginia, Bill Raney is a familiar face. Raney does not mine coal, and he usually appears in a suit and tie, not sooty overalls. But as president of the West Virginia Coal Association, his trim mustache and amiable drawl are instantly recognized in the state capital, where the WVCA wields tremendous influence.

Raney was literally born into the industry. He entered the world in a coal camp called Covel in southern West Virginia, where his father worked for the American Coal Company. The family later moved to nearby Princeton, a town that owes its existence to coal and the railroads that carried it. After college he took a job as a surface coal mine inspector and spent a decade and a half with an earlier industry trade group before joining the coal association in the early 1990s.

"I love the industry, love the people in it," Raney said in a recent interview. "We've seen a lot of transition over the years, but coal's a big part not only of the history of West Virginia but the present, and, we hope, the future."

In 2019, a coal industry organization honored Raney with its Coal Communicator Award to recognize "his great ability to communicate the message of coal to the public."[1]

Much of that message is about just who coal's friends and enemies are. A drive through the state shows how highly successful the association's Friends of Coal campaign has been—billboards, window and bumper stickers, and state-issued license plates all bear the logo.

As for pointing out coal's enemies, that campaign has been pretty successful, too. The "war on coal" has become a mantra for coal country politicians who blame job losses on overzealous environmental regulation. Variations over the years included the "EPA's war on coal" and the "regulatory war on coal." But with the 2008 election, it became "Obama's war on coal."

"Well, we've been through a difficult time," Raney said, "and I'm talking about the Obama administration. They set out at the very beginning, on the first day, we got a letter from the EPA questioning a large [surface mining] permit in southern West Virginia."

In the war-on-coal narrative, it was the Obama administration's efforts to address climate change and rein in the worst effects of mining and burning coal that caused the industry's losses.

Obama assembled a team of environmental champions, including Clinton-era environmental regulator Carol Browner, Nobel laureate Stephen Chu, and others to advise the White House and lead key agencies.[2] Under the administration's leadership, the country took steps to address mining damage to waterways and toxic pollution from coal ash dumps. And with two signature policies—the Clean Power Plan and the Paris Agreement on climate change—the administration aimed to reduce greenhouse gas emissions.

As Raney saw it, those were all direct attacks on his industry.

"They spent eight years trying to put us out of business, not only in West Virginia but across the country. And it's taken its toll," he said.

This rhetoric has been remarkably effective, especially given how factually flawed it is. Numerous independent analyses of the energy industry, and even internal documents from coal company bankruptcy proceedings, show that the main factors driving the industry's decline are market economics, not environmental regulation.

For example, in a 2017 report from Columbia University's Center on Global Energy Policy, researchers analyzed the various factors leading to coal's diminishing share of the electricity market.[3] Competition from cheaper natural gas was the primary factor, accounting for about half of the decline in coal as a fuel. Reduced demand due to increased efficiency and the rise of renewable energy accounted for another 45 percent or so. Environmental regulation was a factor, the researchers said, but a very minor one.[4]

But admitting that coal was simply beaten in a capitalist market is not a strong talking point for the industry.

"It befuddles me," Raney said. "America has more coal than any other country in the world. And the way that a lot of the media and a lot of the environmental groups want us to get out of the coal business totally? It's kind of like if you were in Saudi Arabia and told them to get out of the oil business. I mean, it makes no sense to me."

Donald Trump's 2016 campaign took that industry message to an unprecedented level with his pledges to "end the war on beautiful, clean coal" and put miners back to work.

In May of that election year, shortly after sealing the last required primary votes, Trump rallied in West Virginia's capital, Charleston, surrounded by posters saying "Trump Digs Coal."

"You can't take it, folks," Trump said of his opponent's plans for energy. "You're gonna have your mines closed, 100 percent."

Raney's group presented Trump with a miner's helmet adorned with the Friends of Coal logo.

Trump started to set it on the podium but the crowd chanted for him to put it on. He gingerly placed the helmet atop his signature coif, gave a thumbs-up, and comically pantomimed a digging motion.

"My hair look okay?" Trump asked after taking off the helmet. "I need a little spray."

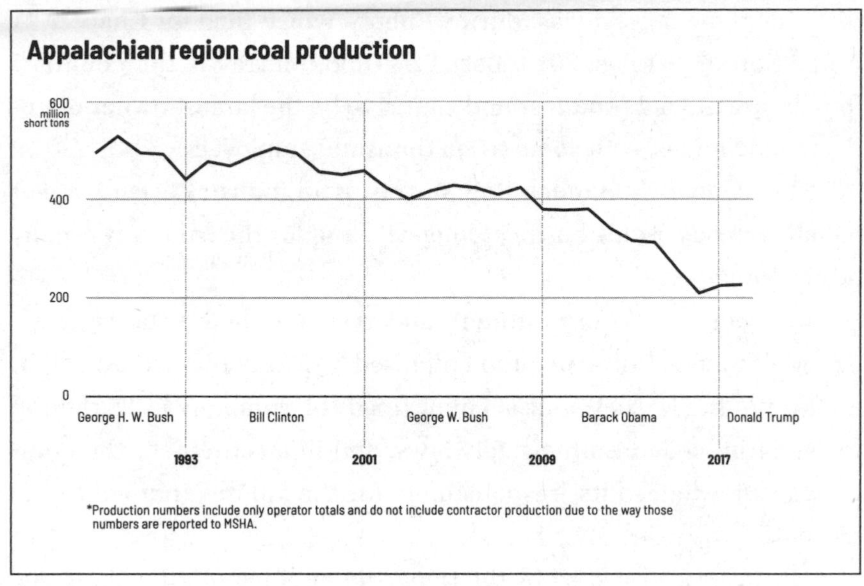

SINCE TRUMP TOOK OFFICE, he has attempted to roll back most of the Obama era's major regulations regarding coal and climate change. The Clean Power Plan, the Paris Agreement, the modest restrictions on toxic coal ash dumps, the protections for streams buried by mining waste—all are gone or greatly weakened.[5]

"If there ever was a war on coal, it is over!" says Trevor Houser, one of the coauthors of the Columbia report. If politicians really believe that those environmental regulations were the culprit in declining coal production, he argued, "then they should expect to see a sharp recovery in coal mining and coal employment in the years ahead."

Of course, apart from a small bump in exports for the coal used in steelmaking, there is no sign of a coal comeback three years into the Trump administration, and government forecasts show further declines through 2020.[6] By the end of 2019, more than half a dozen coal mining companies had declared bankruptcy during the Trump years, most of them in Appalachia.

One of the biggest was Murray Energy, which filed for Chapter 11 protection in October 2019. Based in Ohio, Murray is the country's fourth-largest coal producer and claims to be the largest owner of underground mines, with some seven thousand employees.[7]

The company's founder, Bob Murray, is an industry legend, albeit equally famous for his business longevity and for the company's many mining fatalities.

In August 2007, nine miners and rescuers died after Murray's Crandall Canyon Mine in Utah collapsed.[8] Murray blamed an earthquake, but the Department of Labor fined the company $1.85 million for violating federal mine safety laws, and in a settlement the company acknowledged its "responsibility for the failures that led to the tragedy."

Murray was also sued by the Department of Labor after West Virginia miners complained. The CEO personally told workers in a 2014 meeting to stop making complaints to federal regulators. Under federal law, miners have the right to speak anonymously to government inspectors about mine safety concerns. The court upheld a decision that Murray must personally apologize.[9]

Murray was also a vociferous Obama critic, frequently suing the administration and often taking to cable news shows to rail against the president's energy policies. "What it is is a political power grab of America's power grid to change our country in a diabolical, if not evil, way," he told the *New York Times* in 2016.[10]

Murray is an enthusiastic supporter of President Trump, meeting with him and his cabinet members frequently and donating $300,000 to Trump's inauguration.

Just weeks after Trump took office, Murray shared a detailed "action plan" memo with administration officials. It outlined a series of environmental rollbacks and policy changes that would benefit the US coal industry.

The majority of Murray's wish list—which included the repeal and replacement of the Obama-era Clean Power Plan, withdrawal from the

Paris climate agreement, and staff cuts at the US Environmental Protection Agency—have been carried out.

But that wasn't enough. Murray was still losing market share as coal-burning power plants closed down. So he pushed another proposal to Trump: a massive federal intervention in the electricity markets to force utility companies to purchase coal.

Murray's proposal was premised on protecting the "resiliency" of the nation's electrical grid. Too much reliance on natural gas and renewable energy and a simultaneous loss of the baseload capacity from coal and nuclear power would leave the grid vulnerable to breakdowns and blackouts. Therefore it was in the national interest to ensure a steady stream of power from coal by subsidizing coal.

Trump's Energy Department issued a report on potential threats to grid resiliency, but the report's contents showed that department career analysts were clearly skeptical. The country's largest regional grid operator, PJM Interconnection, which operates across a thirteen-state region including the Ohio Valley, argued that there is no need for such federal intervention.

FERC, the Federal Energy Regulatory Commission, unanimously rejected the proposal.

Just a week before Murray Energy filed for bankruptcy, Bob Murray took to the podium at an event in Lexington, Kentucky, organized by FERC chairman Neil Chatterjee. Murray was not kind to his host.

"The word that I've been using to describe FERC is feckless," Murray told the audience. Inaction by federal regulators, he said, had resulted in "the destruction of America's coal industry, the reliability and resilience of the electric power grid, and the cost of electricity itself."[11]

Murray Energy is a privately held company, so solid information on its operations was not easy to come by. The documentation required by a bankruptcy filing revealed what the company really thought about the direction of the coal industry—a view sharply at odds with Bob Murray's rhetoric.

In one document, the company explains that coal's decline has coincided with the growing affordability of renewable alternatives. Costs for a solar plant decreased by nearly half over five years. Other documents show the company lost export market share, partly due to cheap natural gas exported from the United States to Europe. Ultimately the company expects its coal production to decline another 40 percent in the coming decade.

THE 2016 ELECTION taught us that Appalachia is "Trump Country." Trump took all but 21 of the 420 counties in Appalachia.

Not surprisingly, Trump did especially well in coal-dependent counties. A ReSource analysis of the 2016 vote in Kentucky, Ohio, and West Virginia found the top coal-producing counties typically had wide margins of victory for Trump.[12]

Poor counties also went heavily for Trump. Martin County, for example, with some of the highest poverty in Kentucky, had ten times the vote for Trump than for Clinton. No county in the region with greater than 30 percent poverty went blue. The Appalachian Regional Commission classified fifty-four counties in the three states as economically distressed in 2016. All but one—Athens County, Ohio—went for Trump.

"Our coal jobs are gone here in eastern Kentucky," Judy Collier said from a grocery store parking lot in Whitesburg, Kentucky. She lives in Eolia in Letcher County, which has seen a sharp drop in mine production and employment. "We need jobs," she said, and she liked Trump's focus on bringing coal back.

"I don't think Trump is some savior," Athens County, Ohio, native Rebecca Keller said. "But he is somebody with a different perspective."

"I will keep my fingers crossed that he can effect some real change in this country," steelworker Jack Rose said in Wheeling, West Virginia.

Voter comments like that supported the dominant national narrative about the region's politics: white working-class people voted for Trump out of economic anxiety (or for baser motives).

Frequently, media stories focused on why Trump Country voted "against its own interests"—for a candidate who would reduce access to health care for the poor, cut aid programs, and advance a tax system that favored the idle rich over the working poor.

And while there is some truth to that storyline, it did not adequately explain what ReSource reporters were learning in their communities. Nor did that national narrative square with some of the more striking aspects of the regional voting data.

H. L. Mencken once wrote, “There is always a well-known solution to every human problem—neat, plausible, and wrong.” The national story about our region’s voting seemed just a bit too neat and plausible to be entirely right.

After the election, we noticed a curious trend among many so-called voters we talked to. Quite a few of them hadn’t actually voted. A harder look at the vote totals revealed some striking numbers. In many parts of Trump Country, at least in Appalachia, a lot of people did not vote for Donald Trump. In many cases, they didn’t vote at all.

The *Washington Post* calculated and mapped the percentage of the voting-age population in a given county that voted in 2016. Appalachia stands out as a region where, in many counties, only about half (and often less than half) of those people voted.[13]

The difference is starkest for the coal country of southern West Virginia and eastern Kentucky, which had some of the lowest voter turnout figures in the country. In about forty counties there, fewer than half of adults voted.

One might argue this is due to the effect of the electoral college: the outcome in states like Kentucky and West Virginia was preordained, thus reducing voter turnout. But even in presidential battleground states such as Virginia, Ohio, and Pennsylvania, the Appalachian and coal-producing counties in those states stand out for lower voting rates.

Historian and writer Elizabeth Catte brought early attention to the importance of the Appalachian nonvoters as a counterfactual to the dominant campaign coverage. She found half a dozen examples of national media pieces that used tiny McDowell County in West Virginia’s southern coalfields to explain Trump's appeal to the "forgotten" white working class.

Catte then points out that while, yes, Trump won overwhelmingly in McDowell County, he did so with only about 4,600 votes out of some 17,500 registered voters there. McDowell had the lowest voter turnout of any county in West Virginia, a state with the second-lowest turnout in the country.[14]

Trump Country is probably better described as "none of the above" country.

So why don't more Appalachians vote?

In a report on the 2016 voter turnout, the groups Nonprofit VOTE and the US Elections Project pointed out the importance of state policies, such as online and same-day voter registration, and the effects of gerrymandering.[15] Other voting rights groups point to the increasing number of voting restrictions that target poor and minority voters. These are clearly important factors in parts of Appalachia. Tennessee and West Virginia are both in the bottom five of voter turnout for the past three presidential elections, and both states cut off voter registration weeks before Election Day.

Ohio has strict voting laws, including requirements for voter identification and a controversial use-it-or-lose-it rule on voter registration, which removes people who did not vote in recent elections from the state's rolls. A legal challenge went to the Supreme Court, which upheld Ohio's program in a 5–4 vote in 2018.[16]

Until recently Kentucky was one of just two states that still permanently banned people with past felony criminal convictions from voting. Efforts to expand the vote became ensnared in Kentucky's bitter races for governor, which pitted a father-and-son gubernatorial dynasty against a political outsider.

In the final weeks of his term in 2015, then governor Steve Beshear acted to restore voting rights for those who had completed their sentences for nonviolent crimes. It was a rare area of broad bipartisan agreement, with Senator Rand Paul and the NAACP and ACLU state chapters all celebrating Beshear's executive order.

One month later, however, the newly elected Republican governor, Matt Bevin, reversed Beshear's order and brought back the voting ban—once again making Kentucky "a national outlier for disenfranchising citizens with past criminal convictions," according to the Brennan Center for Justice.[17]

The *Lexington Herald-Leader* estimated that about 180,000 Kentuckians were disenfranchised because of this, and a Department of Justice review estimated that this law affects one in five black adults in Kentucky.

In 2019, Steve Beshear's son, Andy Beshear, narrowly defeated Bevin. In his first week as governor, he announced he would return to his father's policy and expand voting rights for some former offenders.

But even those barriers, while troubling, do not fully explain Appalachia's remarkably low voter participation. Perhaps the strongest explanation in social science is one that's frequently overlooked: the correlation between low voter turnout and high levels of poverty and inequality.

In their acclaimed 2009 book *The Spirit Level*, British epidemiologists Richard Wilkinson and Kate Pickett explored a range of social and health ills that are connected to income inequality, including low measures of civic trust and civic participation. By Wilkinson and Pickett's reckoning, several Appalachian states rank among the most unequal in the United States. They find Kentucky and West Virginia have some of the highest rates of inequality and the lowest levels of civic trust.

(By contrast, when asked "Would you fare well in a fistfight?" Wilkinson and Pickett found that people in West Virginia tend to say yes.)

Researchers at the University of Essex in the United Kingdom found that geographic isolation among the poor leads to lower voter turnout.[18] And work at the University of Texas linked higher income inequality to lower voter turnout and found that "higher levels of economic segregation" are also associated with depressed turnout.[19]

Other studies find that people with lower socioeconomic status are the least likely to vote in an election and "tend to withdraw" from political activity. They are "less likely to volunteer for a political campaign, contact a political official, attend a political meeting or wear a political campaign button," social psychologist Jazmin Brown-Iannuzzi and her colleagues wrote in a 2016 paper.[20]

Brown-Iannuzzi taught at the University of Kentucky at the time, and is now at the University of Virginia. She said the research on inequality and voting is mixed, but the link between low voting and low socioeconomic status is strong. The reasons may be as mundane as the inability to get time off from work to vote or a lack of transportation to the polling place.

"So, even though voting is intended to be inclusive to all citizens, there still exist objective financial barriers for lower [income] citizens," she said.

Brown-Iannuzzi pointed out that some studies have linked high inequality with support for authoritarianism. A 2019 study across voters in several countries suggests that when economic inequality is high, people prefer a "strong leader," even at the expense of democracy. Other studies link high inequality with greater interpersonal distrust and reduced support for democracy in general. High inequality is associated with desire for an authoritarian leader who disregards party politics.

"It may be that in contexts of high inequality, people want a leader who is seen as an 'outsider,'" Brown-Iannuzzi said, "because the traditional approaches are seen as part of the problem that created the current situation of high inequality."

IN THE 1970S, a young student at Vanderbilt University in Nashville set out for the Clear Fork Valley, an area straddling the border between Tennessee's eastern counties and the southeastern corner of Kentucky.

John Gaventa would soon be leaving for the UK on a Rhodes scholarship, but first he had work to do here, where his family had deep roots. He was exploring two of the defining characteristics of Appalachian coal country, which often seemed at odds. Why did extreme poverty persist among people who were sitting atop enormous mineral wealth? And why were those people not voting to change such a glaring injustice?

"You know, I had been taught in political science that if the citizens had a grievance, if they got mad and were in a free country, they would organize and they would have their voice heard," Gaventa said in an interview with the ReSource. "But when I went to that region, I was really struck by the lack of action."

Gaventa had volunteered in the area on earlier projects, including an influential study of Appalachian land ownership. He found that the bulk of local wealth was owned by a handful of distant companies that paid little in local taxes and did not reinvest in local communities. That helped to solve the first paradox of poverty amid wealth: the wealth had simply gone elsewhere. But why, then, did people not vote to change that?

Gaventa's deep study of the history and social dynamics of the Clear Fork Valley resulted in a landmark work titled *Power and Powerlessness*. He found a strong link between economic inequality and political quiescence.

"The patterns of economic inequality translated themselves into patterns of political inequality, and inequalities of power and voice," he wrote, patterns that have come to dictate how people engage in politics.

Lately Gaventa has been taking a fresh look at the region where he did that work. Amid growing disillusionment with institutions and loss of trust in political leaders, he argues, many assumptions about voting behavior no longer apply.

"The notion of 'Trump Country' doesn't hold," he said, in part because of that huge chunk of Appalachians who didn't vote. "The key point is that nonparticipation can be just as important an indicator of behavior as is participation."

Politicians and pundits have ignored a vital clue: the dog that didn't bark.

This extreme level of nonvoting is telling us something important, he says, and is linked to similar patterns in other parts of the world. Gaventa says this reflects growing disillusionment with the whole notion that voting can bring about change and a deep loss of trust in political leaders and political institutions.

As long ago as the 1980s, Gaventa coined the word "Appalachianization" to describe the loss of trust, the loss of jobs and opportunity, the declining social capital, and the decaying infrastructure long associated with Appalachia that have become common across larger parts of rural America.

Take a look at the data on rural areas over the last twenty years, he said, and you find unemployment affecting large parts of the rural heartland. The Economic Innovation Group, which produces an index of distressed communities, has called this the "ruralization of distress." While the overall number of people living in distressed areas declined, the number of rural Americans living in distress has gone up sharply.

Instead of thinking of places like Appalachia as being left behind, Gaventa said, we need to think of them as "being sort of the canaries in the mine, of what other parts of the world are becoming like."

That means more parts of America where the bulk of wealth rests in fewer hands, where locals lack control over resources, and where inequalities in political power reach extreme levels.

Yet even amid this rising distress and declining trust, he sees different kinds of civic engagement bubbling up. Communities that have been "on the sharp edge of inequality" are now mobilizing for alternatives.

"I'm struck by the enormous amount of local civic activism and new forms of civic activism that's occurring," he said. "People are acting and resisting, but in very different ways."

He sees it when miners occupy railroad tracks, when teachers strike for better pay and better schools, when activists block new gas pipelines, when young people who had left the region return to try something new in their old hometowns. And so Gaventa has found a third Appalachian paradox to puzzle out.

"There's a contradiction here between the low levels of political participation that go one way, and then the deep levels of citizen-based activities that imply a different kind of understanding of what's going on."

PROFILE:
Carl and Scott Shoupe

WHEN THE BERNIE SANDERS campaign came to Kentucky in the summer of 2019, it was on the heels of the release of Sanders's ambitious climate change plan. His version of the Green New Deal included a list of policies for coal communities that progressive Appalachian activists had been advocating for decades. The plan's call for sharp reductions in the use of fossil fuels could kneecap what's left of the region's coal industry, but it would fund programs to help coal-reliant communities make a transition to a more just economy. Carl and Scott Shoupe were on the shortlist of Kentuckians the Sanders campaign wanted at their Louisville rally. Carl and Scott are a father-son duo from perhaps the most famous coal mining region in the country: Harlan County.

Together or separately, the pair have testified in Congress about strip-mining, helped the Kentucky Coal Museum go solar, lobbied politicians for funding for black lung disease, and been featured in national media outlets.

Their story is in some ways utterly typical. Carl, the elder Shoupe, followed his father's footsteps into coal mining in the early 1960s, and Scott, in turn, followed his father Carl underground in the 1990s. But in other ways, they've traced an entirely new path that says a great deal about the future of the region they call home.

Carl became a union organizer after a mining accident left him unable to go back underground. Now retired, he's a vocal member of the progressive group Kentuckians for the Commonwealth. His son, Scott, climbed the ranks in the mining industry, eventually overseeing dozens of miners in multiple states before his disillusionment with the industry's treatment of workers led him to quit. He's now the proprietor of New Age Solutions, where he helps businesses and residents make smarter energy choices.

The Shoupes have lived in Harlan County for generations. The family's responses to the booms and busts of the coal industry show how one industry shaped whole communities over the course of decades.

Carl was born in 1946, in the coal camp of Lynch, Kentucky. Back in those days, Lynch was the biggest coal town in the nation, home to the biggest coal tipple. Carl was proud of that tipple, and he was proud of men like his father, Buck, who worked some thirty years for U.S. Steel.

According to a 2009 book on coal camp baseball leagues, Buck was known as "the meanest man in Harlan County." Author Lynn Sutter wrote that Buck "would leave his home for long periods of time to preach the UMWA gospel throughout the coalfields, frequently under an alias. Arrested at the Battle of Evarts, he was tried, convicted, and served time on a charge of 'banding and confederating.'"[1]

Later, Buck would gift his young son the revolver he'd carried during that battle. "I don't know if he killed any of those guys," Carl said, "but he was firing his weapon at those scabs and those gun thugs."

U.S. Steel was growing so fast it couldn't find enough workers in eastern Kentucky, Carl said. "So they went up to Ellis Island and put on a big spiel, and in Lynch in the early 1950s, there were something like ten thousand people that lived in this camp," he said. And among those ten thousand were people from dozens of different ethnic groups. "You look at it now and you say, 'How in the world could ten

Scott Shoupe followed his father into the mining industry. Today both work to help their community find a new path forward. "It is inevitable that coal's coming to an end," he said.

thousand have lived in this place?' But there were houses built all over the place back then."

By the time Carl was born, U.S. Steel, Lynch Division, had signed a contract with the UMWA. Miners got better pay, eight-hour shifts, weekends off. But the company retained its stranglehold on every aspect of miners' lives. U.S. Steel owned Lynch. It built the roads. It owned Carl's house in No. 2 Camp. On Friday, Buck would get his paycheck from U.S. Steel, and on Saturday he'd spend that paycheck back at U.S. Steel's barbershop and beer hall and company store.

"U.S. Steel wanted all their employees living in the camp," Carl went on. "I have to say it: they ran a pretty tight ship. If a miner got out of hand, got drunk, maybe some domestic violence on the weekend, on

Monday morning that dude would be packed and gone. They had security men that would come around and check everything."

On his walk to school, Carl would stop outside Portal 31 to admire the coal-smudged men emerging from the mine, disappearing into the U.S. Steel bathhouse, and emerging once again freshly scrubbed and cleaned. He'd watch the men amble across the street to the U.S. Steel restaurant, which had one door for black miners and one door for white miners. He'd peer down Silk Stocking Street, which is what boys like him called the area where the elites, the wealthy supervisors from Pittsburgh, lived apart from their employees.

But the golden days of Carl's childhood didn't last long. By the time he was fourteen years old, in 1960, technology had improved, and it took fewer men to run a mine. There were massive layoffs. As Appalachians went north to the factories in Detroit, Indianapolis, and Chicago, U.S. Steel razed its empty coal camps to the ground.

Buck Shoupe was laid off that year. "I didn't realize it, but looking back, my dad was thought of good by the company, so my dad had the opportunity to be called back if the mines got going again." When U.S. Steel destroyed No. 2 Camp, the company gave the Shoupes a new home on Main Street.

During Carl's four years of high school, Buck was out of work. He made ends meet by digging through the rubble of Lynch's razed camps, scavenging for copper and steel.

"When I got out of high school, I went in the Marine Corps," Carl said. He was deployed in Vietnam, he said, for "thirteen months and four days, twelve hours, and twenty-seven minutes." He doesn't talk about it now, but he still works with the Veterans Administration on his flashbacks.

All of Carl's classmates had gone into the war together, and they all arrived back in Harlan County at around the same time. "We all got together and we started running around, just trying to forget where we'd come from. Man, we stayed drunk for two months, three months. It was so much fun." After a brief stint in Louisville working a factory job, Carl returned to Harlan County as a roof bolter for U.S. Steel.

Within a year, he was caught in a mine cave-in. He was trapped under a boulder "the size of a pool table," he told Sutter, that left him in the hospital, in a full-body cast, for over a year, and in rehab for two years after that. The wounds healed, but his body still echoes with the injuries he sustained in that cave-in. He didn't go back underground. Instead, he followed in his father's footsteps and became a strike organizer for the UMWA.

"U.S. Steel and the union worked so closely together, they got along real good," Carl said. "Even though I got hurt myself, U.S. Steel was a safe mine; they preached safety. U.S. Steel, Lynch District, never did have a disaster. They'd have fatalities every now and then, but not many of those, considering the number of men who worked in those mines."

Carl met the woman who would become his wife, Pequita, at a youth center in Cumberland. The pair would have three children, two boys and a girl.

Scott Shoupe was the middle child. He remembers Lynch as a place where you respected your elders, a "yes-sir-no-sir" kind of place, a place where you have only what you work for. "I think that's a lot of mountain people's culture. There's a lot of love and family culture that I was raised in, which is common for this area."

Scott remembers the tri-cities, as he calls them, as "booming, magnificent little towns." In the summer, he'd spend his days at one of the two swimming pools, and in the winter, he and the boys from the neighborhood would play coal miner in the basement, using their dads' old helmets and flashlights and whatever odd mining tools they could find around the house.

But Scott was aware, from the age of seven or so, that the coal industry was in decline. He attended the Lynch school, then the Benham school, then the Cumberland school, as Harlan County's population dwindled and schools consolidated. He remembers waves of sadness as friend after friend moved away.

All of Scott's baseball and football coaches came to games still smudged black from the mines. But by the time he was in high school, those same men were out of work, trying to get jobs as janitors in the school system, or trying to earn degrees, or just moving away.

Scott got into mining right after he got his associate's degree. Just like his father, Scott went each morning to the same mine, asking again and again to be hired until finally the company took him on.

"You know, my dad and I had really similar stories, except I guess we had different addictions," Scott said. "My dad was a functioning alcoholic for, I mean, heck, most of my life. Not that he ever was bad or mistreated us—he worked all the time, but he also drank all the time. If he wasn't working, he was drinking. He was never mean, he never lost employment over it, but he was a hundred-percent functioning alcoholic."

Carl drank to forget Vietnam, and he drank to forget his mining injury. Scott, on the other hand, started taking pills in high school and running with the wrong crowd, for less clear reasons.

"When I started in 1995, the coal industry was kind of transitioning out of unions," Scott said. "The union had become, like everything else, so business-oriented and had fallen away from what's truly right for employees versus companies."

Scott worked his way up, taking on more and more responsibility until he was overseeing safety compliance for dozens of mines.

"I never gave no true thought into what we done as far as the emissions and pollution we put into the atmosphere. I always went to work and looked at the coal industry as a job to support my family. [But] I was never really a true part of raising my kids, because I spent so much time away."

Throughout his time as a miner and a mine supervisor, Scott continued to abuse pills and other drugs. He stole his mother Pequita's jewelry and sold it for drug money. He wrote bad checks, got caught, and served time for the felony. But as far as Carl is concerned, the worst thing Scott ever did, his son's only unforgivable act, was to sell the little pistol Buck Shoupe had carried in the Battle of Evarts in 1931.

Still, despite watching the industry contract, Scott stuck with it. In December 2012, Alpha Coal laid off 3,500 employees in Kentucky and southwest Virginia. "I personally handed out thousands of layoff slips at multiple different operations. But it was never a thought in my mind that I wouldn't retire from the coal industry."

But the higher Scott rose in the ranks of the mining industry, the more disillusioned he felt by the industry's focus on profit over worker safety. He felt pressured to cut corners and put workers at risk. Finally, in 2018, he quit.

It took Scott a long time to figure out what to do next, but he knew he could no longer ignore the environmental impact his work was having or the workers and nearby residents it put at risk.

In 2018, Scott signed up for an internship with the Mountain Association for Community and Economic Development. The program was designed to help displaced coal miners find work in renewable energy and energy efficiency. Within a year, Scott had his own business, New Age Solutions. He was the exclusive energy auditor for the energy efficiency retrofit program Benham$aves. And he was finding new ways to talk to miners he had worked with for years about the future.

"It is inevitable that coal's coming to an end, and it is inevitable that we have to—not today, but yesterday—get something moving in the right direction for people in this area."

Today, Carl Shoupe likes to drink his coffee and eat his breakfast croissant at Lamp House Coffee in Lynch, Kentucky. The café has two doors. Once, the Lamp House was a restaurant owned by U.S. Steel; one of those doors was for black miners, and one was for white miners. Across the street, Portal 31 has been turned into a museum. Just down the road, what was once the country's largest coal tipple stands idle, but beside it, there are rows and rows of brand-new solar panels, signaling that even if Carl and Scott are outliers, the Harlan County tri-cities are not far behind them.

11.
Coal, Climate, and Just What "Just Transition" Means

DANNY FERGUSON DIDN'T like what he saw happening in Lincoln County, the part of southern West Virginia where he grew up. Young people had few job options beyond some fast-food places.

"We don't have nothing else for them to be employed," Ferguson said. "I'd see all these kids with no possibilities, couldn't get a job, because everywhere they'd apply they'd say they want two to five years experience. Well, how you gonna get the experience if no one will hire you?"

That's a common conundrum for those first entering the workforce, but in a rural, economically distressed county it's an even greater challenge. Lincoln County has a poverty rate of 23 percent; it has lost about 5 percent of its population over the past decade.[1]

"Lincoln County is in bad shape," Ferguson said. "Coalfield seemed like the only one willing to take a chance in that area."

That's the Coalfield Development Corporation, a nonprofit where Ferguson worked as a crew chief to mentor and train young people in carpentry and other skills. Trainees earn pay while getting experience as they take on a range of work, from reclaiming old buildings to restoring furniture and even installing solar energy systems.[2]

Ferguson said the program offers hope in an otherwise bleak situation. "The coal is dead, but they're trying to find something for these kids to go do instead of nothing," he said. "That's the whole reason I took this job."

Ferguson sat with one of his young trainees, Jacob Dyer, as they looked at some photos from some of their recent projects. Building the foundation for a solar facility had been a tough but rewarding job. Both were splattered with mud in the pictures, and the strain of the work showed on their faces.

"It was a rough day that day. We was behind the gun," Ferguson remembered.

He and other mentors teach young people like Dyer how to install solar panels and other electrical work. It's one way Coalfield Development is trying to support a more diverse economy and give young workers like Dyer opportunities closer to home.

Danny Ferguson (left) and Jacob Dyer on a Coalfield Development Corporation work training site. "The coal is dead, but they're trying to find something for these kids to go do instead of nothing," Ferguson said.

"I'd prefer to stay here," Dyer said, "stay home and be around my family. And help the economy, you know?"

Coalfield Development launched about a decade ago, primarily to address rural housing issues. Today, crew members like Dyer get a mix of on-the-job training, community college and business classes, and personal development coaching.

Dyer also worked on the renovation of some low-income apartments nearby. He thought about what it would be like to drive by it someday, maybe with his child.

"If you build something that's still there years later, it's a sense of pride," he said.

Ferguson's crew is in the process of transforming an abandoned factory into a training center. He said the property, once a haven for drug use and vagrancy, will now become a positive force for the community.

"It sums up what Coalfield stands for," Ferguson said. "What other people are giving up on, we are not giving up on. One way or another, we will make it happen."

IN PAINTSVILLE, KENTUCKY, another coal town not far away, Melissa Anderson was getting a different kind of job training.

"This is one that I created while we were doing JavaScript," Anderson said, demonstrating a smartphone app she developed to show weather by ZIP code. Anderson was in a program called TechHire Eastern Kentucky, which offers coding classes and job-placement services.[3] Just a year earlier, Anderson was unemployed, trying to keep her home from falling into foreclosure.

"I built it," she said. "And, you know, for me to lose that home would have been devastating."

Anderson was among more than eight hundred people who applied for a little more than fifty trainee positions with TechHire, which aimed to jump-start tech jobs and diversify the job base in the area.

The program had mixed results overall, but it worked for Anderson. She got a job with Interapt, a Louisville-based tech company. And she's happy to report that she's caught up on her mortgage payments.

TechHire and the Coalfield Development Corporation are among the dozens of community and economic development organizations operating in the region, thanks in part to support from the Appalachian Regional Commission. The ARC has been funding infrastructure and economic development projects since its creation more than fifty years ago as part of Lyndon Johnson's Great Society program.

Throughout its history, the ARC has faced criticism from both flanks. Some point to the persistence of Appalachian poverty over half a century, especially in coal-dependent communities, as evidence that the commission has failed by not investing enough or in the right places.

Others say the ARC spends too much. President Trump's first budget proposal, for example, would have eliminated ARC funding entirely.[4] Congressional supporters pushed back, as they have in the past when other presidents proposed cutting the commission and questioned whether its mission was still worthwhile.

Today, the fate of coal country could well depend on what role the ARC plays. Tim Thomas is one of the people who will determine that role.

A Kentucky native and former staffer for the Senate majority leader, Mitch McConnell, Thomas was appointed the ARC's "federal co-chair" in 2018.[5] If it seems an unusual title, that's because the ARC is an unusual organization. There's an old joke that the platypus is an animal designed by committee. Well, the ARC might just be the platypus of federal agencies.

The ARC came about amid a wariness of federal power and a willingness to spend federal dollars, so there's a lot of state-federal power sharing inherent in its design. The commission comprises fourteen members, thirteen of them the governors of the Appalachian states; the fourteenth is the federal co-chair—now Tim Thomas.

Shortly after taking the position, Thomas told the ReSource that his vision for the ARC is "to see the day that this agency can shutter its doors, because its goals and objectives have been reached in large measure."

That day has not come, as the ARC's own data on distressed economies clearly shows. And with the combination of coal's collapse and a raging addiction crisis pushing many communities and local governments toward fiscal freefall, the ARC's role is arguably as critical as ever.

The commission's main tool is an Obama-era program called the POWER Initiative; it's an acronym for Partnerships for Opportunity and Workforce and Economic Revitalization.

POWER was initially part of a larger Obama proposal that included protections for miners' pensions and health benefits, investment in carbon capture and storage technology, and more than $1 billion in spending for economic development and environmental restoration.[6]

Much of that agenda still languishes in Congress, in bills that have been introduced repeatedly and unsuccessfully. The part that Congress did fund was $200 million to be parceled out over four years in grants for various projects aimed at revitalizing places hard-hit by the loss of coal jobs and revenue.

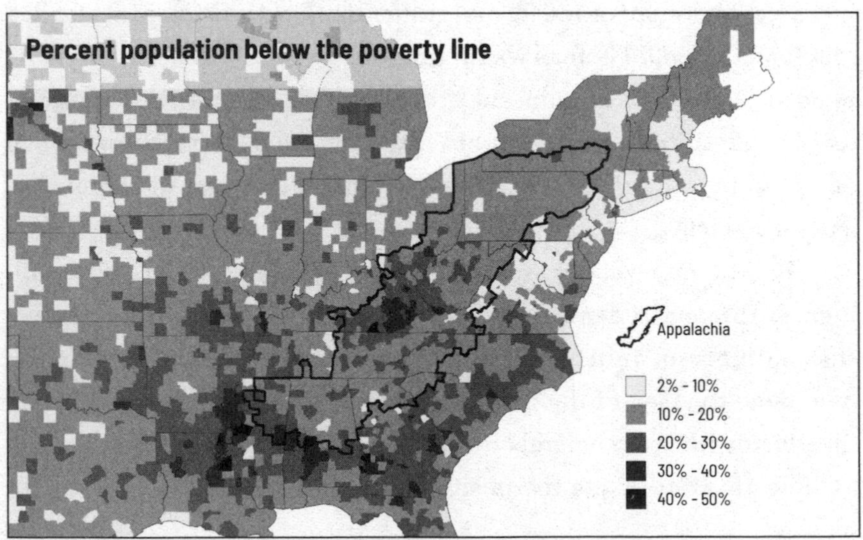

As of late 2019, the initiative had invested some $190 million in more than three hundred coal-affected communities.[7] That seems like a lot—until you consider that in just a few small, rural counties alone, local officials are staring down revenue losses of tens of millions of dollars that once supported schools and other vital services. Given that scale of need, Thomas acknowledges that the POWER Initiative is not up to the task of a transition away from coal.

"Ah, probably not," he said in an interview. "But it wasn't really supposed to be. That was the ARC helping to soften the blow of the decline in the coal industry."

Thomas said the commission's purpose with the POWER grants, and indeed its purpose all along, has been to leverage other funds—a sort of federal source of seed money.

"We'd like to see other folks commit their resources, certainly at the local level. We like to see our dollars leverage other dollars."

So far, the commission estimated that the POWER grants have leveraged more than $811 million in additional investment.

Thomas said that, since its founding, the ARC has funded construction of some three thousand miles of highways, which he called a "transformational" infrastructure development. And over the broader sweep of the ARC's work, poverty levels across the region have dropped dramatically. In 1960, about three hundred Appalachian counties were high-poverty areas, he said. Today they number fewer than a hundred.

"But while that number has shrunk, it's kind of shrunk toward this persistent area right in the middle," he said, referring to what he called "the most challenging areas" in central Appalachia's coal country.

Thomas blamed the region's geography, in part. "It's difficult to attract outside investment in areas with challenging terrain." But others offer a different explanation for why this area has remained so poor for so long.

"To a great degree, the war on poverty did more to enhance and benefit the middle class than it ever did to restructure and provide benefits for the poor," historian Ron Eller said in an interview.

A professor emeritus at the University of Kentucky's Appalachian Center, Eller spent much of his forty-year career studying the region. He also has ancestors going back some eight generations in Appalachia, a family history that he said reflects the upheaval and economic dislocation that defined the area. He was the first in that long line to go to college.

"I wanted to really try to understand the roots of the economic conditions here," he said. "So that's why I became a historian."

In his 2008 book *Uneven Ground*, Eller provides a trenchant critique of the ARC, arguing that the commission and its leaders failed to tackle the most important underlying structural issues contributing to Appalachian poverty.

As Thomas noted, the ARC seeks to invest where it can leverage other funding. Eller traced this to the commission's founding language: investments "shall be concentrated in areas where there is a significant potential for future growth" and where the expected return on public dollars invested will be the greatest.[8]

This instruction was meant to ease congressional concerns about giving local control over spending to politicians in a region famous, at the time, for corruption. But Eller argues that the long-term effect was to steer money toward populated "growth poles" that looked promising rather than to directly aid the counties and communities in greatest need.

The ARC has followed the precept in the old saying that the Good Lord helps those who help themselves. And the places at the wealthier margins of the Appalachian region have certainly helped themselves—to the lion's share of early ARC funding.

Eller wrote that a decade into the ARC's mission, about 77 percent of commission funding flowed to the extreme northern and southern parts of the region, which are closer to major population centers. Less than a quarter went to central Appalachia, which had—and still has—the deepest poverty.[9] By the mid-1970s, he wrote, the ARC was widely considered a boondoggle that had done little to alleviate poverty in the regions it was created to help.

Eller recognizes the importance of the ARC's investment in roads, medical centers, community colleges, and the like. But much as the ARC placed its investment bets at the geographic margins of Appalachia, poverty programs like it largely worked at the edges of the issues rather than on the core causes of poverty and inequality.

"We need to understand development in a different kind of way," Eller said. That would begin with a recognition that Appalachia is fully American, "an inherent component of that larger society," he said. "Things in the mountains aren't going to change until we begin to address some of those larger issues nationally."

Eller sees income inequality, health disparities, and looming environmental crises pushing Appalachia and America together toward a reckoning. Perhaps the greatest catalyst for that is our changing climate and the effects that people are starting to feel in all parts of the country, including coal country.

"THAT WAS LIKE the night from hell," Susan Jack said. The night in question was June 23, 2016, when Jack's town of Clendenin, along the Elk River north of Charleston, was rapidly disappearing under water.[10]

"It just came up so fast that you really didn't have a whole lot of time to respond," she said. "I ended up carrying my ninety-year-old great-aunt through floodwaters that night to get out."

Some eight to ten inches of rain fell on West Virginia's steep hills and narrow valleys over about twelve hours. Most of the state was under an emergency declaration. Twenty-three people died, making it the deadliest flash flood in the country in fifteen years.

Meteorologists use a measure called annual exceedance probabilities to give a sense of how heavy rainfall events compare to statistical expectations. A really big storm might produce a hundred-year event—something you would expect to happen only once a century. The 2016 storm was a thousand-year event in some parts of the state.

The following summer, eight West Virginia counties were again under a state of emergency due to flash flooding from heavy downpours. Next door in Kentucky, there have been sixteen federally declared major disasters in the past ten years, most due to flooding, according to a review of FEMA data by the Center for Public Integrity.[11] Half were in just one county, Pike County, the "energy capital" in the state's eastern coalfields.

In the summer of 2010, Janie Caudill was on vacation in Tennessee when a flash flood swept through the holler along Pike County's Harless Creek, where she lives. When she got the news she raced home, stopping only to buy rain boots.

"The flood was so big that there was no road to walk on, so we had to go through the mountains," she said.

Caudill's hair salon was completely destroyed. She turned to the Small Business Administration to help rebuild. "I ended up borrowing $90,000, and I've got a payment now till I'm ninety-two," she said with a laugh.

A year after the flooding disaster that hit Susan Jack's home in West Virginia, she and her neighbors were still working to get back to something approaching normal. She joined the local committee on long-term recovery, a job they expected to take another few years.

"Unless you've been through this, you just don't get it. You don't have a clue," she said. "I lost everything."

Climate scientists say these flooding disasters are made more likely by a warming climate. "Data are very clear," said Michael Mann, professor of atmospheric science at Penn State University. "There is a substantial increase in what we call the intensity of rainfall events, which is simply to say flooding—more extreme and more prevalent flooding."

The National Climate Assessment report, compiled by NOAA, the National Oceanic and Atmospheric Administration, with some three hundred experts contributing, shows that intense rainstorms have increased significantly in central Appalachia over the past half century.[12]

For West Virginia, the proportion of precipitation that comes down in the heaviest storms went up by 71 percent in that period.[13] Just from the 1990s to the 2000s, those heavy downpours increased by 50 percent.[14] The pattern is consistent with warming, scientists say, and climate forecasts show a strong likelihood that those trends will continue as the planet warms further.

Mann said it's useful to think of the atmosphere as a sponge that can hold more moisture as it gets warmer. "When you squeeze that sponge you're going to get more intense rainfall events, more intense flooding," he said. "And the data indicate that this is indeed happening."

And yet, opposition to action on climate change is nearly universal for the region's members of Congress. It's a position that cuts across party lines in coal country, where proposals to reduce emissions are viewed as existential threats.

Governors and attorneys general of both parties in Kentucky, Ohio, and West Virginia joined the states who successfully sued the Obama administration over the EPA Clean Power Plan, which would have required some reductions in CO_2 emissions from power plants.[15] Patrick Morrisey, attorney general for West Virginia, later made it a central part of his Republican bid for the US Senate.

But the pro-coal stance didn't help Morrisey differentiate himself from the Democratic incumbent, Senator Joe Manchin, who won handily. Manchin had long ago staked out the coal territory.

In one of the most famous demonstrations of fossil fuel fealty, Manchin's 2010 Senate campaign ad showed him in hunting gear near a printout labeled CAP AND TRADE. This was while congressional leaders of his own party were considering major climate legislation, including a cap-and-trade approach to rein in greenhouse gas emissions.

"I'll take dead aim at the cap-and-trade bill," Manchin said to the camera, then loaded a cartridge into the chamber, sighted up, and shot dead center through that menacing pile of paper. "Because it's bad for West Virginia."

But some of the most sophisticated available public opinion research on the issue indicates that political leaders in the region are out of step with their constituents on climate change.

It's difficult and costly to get good public opinion data across the entire country. Anthony Leiserowitz and his team at the Yale Program on Climate Change Communication devised a method using sophisticated models based on a range of predictive demographic factors.[16] They spot-tested results against independent surveys and found their models are about 98 percent accurate.

And what the models show is revelatory. In every Appalachian state, a majority of people think that global warming is happening, that the government should support renewable energy research, and that fossil fuel companies should pay a tax on CO_2. Fifty-six percent of Kentuckians say the government should set strict CO_2 limits on coal power stations.[17]

"There's support for this transition from a fossil fuel industry to a clean-energy industry in West Virginia!" Leiserowitz said. "Not as strong as in, say, Rhode Island, but still a clear majority of folks."

BUT MIXED WITH that support is tremendous anxiety about how that change would affect a place so strongly associated with fossil fuels. Barring some game-changing breakthrough in the technology of carbon capture and storage, sometimes called "clean coal," any significant policy to reduce greenhouse gas emissions will dramatically lower coal use, and natural gas as well.

"And so it got us to thinking," Adele Morris said. "Shouldn't we be thinking ahead to what this means for the state and local governments?"

Morris is policy director for the Climate and Energy Economics Project at the Brookings Institution. In 2019, she and her colleagues looked at some scenarios for what might happen to local governments in coal country under different climate policies. The report's title is a bit of a spoiler: "The Risk of Fiscal Collapse in Coal-Reliant Communities."[18]

When mines close, workers are dislocated and tax revenue dries up, forcing cuts in education and basic services. People move away and home prices fall, further eroding the tax base. Social problems mount, while officials have fewer resources to address them.

"Then you get sort of this death spiral," Morris said, "and there's really no good way for the local government to get back on its feet."

Under some policy scenarios, aggressive action to address climate change could well be the final nail in the coffin for communities that depend on coal. But some of the scarier outcomes outlined in the report are already a reality for many of those local governments.

The Brookings report identifies Boone County, in the southern coalfields of West Virginia, as among the local governments most highly dependent on coal.

In just the past five years, coal production has declined in Boone County by about 70 percent, with twenty of the thirty-one mines in the county closing down. The county closed three of its elementary schools and, despite emergency funding from the state, still had to cut back other basic services.

For Boone County and many other coal-dependent communities, the fiscal death spiral is already underway—or at least close enough for folks to feel its gravitational pull.

Some Boone County organizations won money from the Appalachian Regional Commission's POWER grants, and some locals and leaders of the state's congressional delegation support the RECLAIM Act. That bill would expand the type of work that could receive money from the federal Abandoned Mine Land Fund. But compared to the scale of challenges counties like Boone are up against, Morris is skeptical that those programs would be enough to make a difference.

"My own view, though, is those are kind of small potatoes compared with what's really necessary," she said. "I think we really need something in the billions of dollars per year invested in these communities."

And where would such levels of funding come from?

"Let's just say we had a carbon tax," Morris proposed, something like \$25 per ton of CO_2 or its equivalent. Her report's modeling projects that with a roughly 5 percent annual increase for inflation, such a tax would generate revenue on the order of *$1 trillion* over the first ten years.

"That kind of revenue allows for a very generous support for coal-reliant areas," she said, outlining a program that could put tens of billions of dollars toward halting the fiscal slide and empowering a transition to a new economic base.

"I think we need to think a little bit bigger about what the real needs are and what the right kind of instruments are to serve them," Morris said.

The very thing that seemed like the death knell for coal country—ambitious legislation to address climate change—could instead become its saving grace. This is part of the thinking behind proposals such as the much-discussed Green New Deal.

These plans generally include some mechanism to direct revenue generated from the cap on greenhouse gas emissions—such as the carbon tax Morris outlined—into a "just transition" for coal country and other places affected by the power switch.

That idea has been a part of climate policy thinking for decades now. But getting consensus on just what a just transition should include is a big task.

The Climate Justice Alliance, which includes about seventy community and environmental justice groups from around the country, says we must take a "whole-society approach" to climate change.[19] The group has already sounded a note of concern about the Green New Deal, arguing that it was rolled out in a "grass *tops*" fashion, without adequate input from groups in affected communities. As a cautionary tale, they cited the last major climate legislation and its ill-fated slog up Capitol Hill.

Congressional representatives Henry Waxman (now retired) and Ed Markey (now a senator) successfully shepherded their American Clean Energy and Security Act, or ACES, through the House in 2009, with strong support from national environmental groups.

But, says the Climate Justice Alliance, the green coalition did not do enough to address the needs and concerns of working-class people and communities along the fence lines of America's energy system. As a result, the climate bill did not get the support and momentum needed to overcome the substantial opposition (and filibuster threshold) in the Senate.

The ACES bill was the legislation that Senator Manchin went gunning for in his campaign ad. As it turned out, no rifle shot was required. The bill died in the Senate without a full floor vote.

Hillary Clinton's 2016 run for president also offered a stark example of how hard it is to turn the idea of a coal country transition into something that works in a political campaign. Clinton had a robust and detailed plan for the transition. But at a campaign event in Ohio, her attempt to communicate it gave her opponents a gift in the form of a gaffe. Explaining her plan to bring clean-energy jobs to coal country, she added a line that would become fodder for countless attack ads: "We're going to put a lot of coal miners and coal companies out of business."[20]

It was clear, in context, that she was not expressing a desire to put miners out of work. Rather, she was talking about the need to buffer against such an event, whether the loss of jobs came as a result of government energy policy or energy market trends.

Clinton even followed that line with a statement that we should not forget those who "labored in those mines for generations, losing their health, often losing their lives to turn on our lights and power our factories."

But, as always, context is the first casualty of political campaigns.

At a round table event in West Virginia an unemployed miner named Bo Copley confronted Clinton. "How you can say you're gonna put a lot of coal miners out of jobs, and then come in here and tell us how you're gonna be our friend?" After that, the narrative was set.

In her 2017 book about the campaign, *What Happened*, Clinton called her statement about miners one of the things "I regret the most."[21]

In the 2020 election, the Democrats' divide between blue-collar workers and green-group agendas has the potential to once again become a major fault line. Republicans have seized on the Green New Deal as a new red menace, and some labor groups are wary of the promise of a just transition.

"First of all, there's never been a 'just transition' in the history of America, which is a pretty bold statement, but a very accurate statement," UMWA president Cecil Roberts said in an interview with the ReSource. "So the odds are not with us, are they?"

There may be useful lessons in how some other countries have approached large-scale changes in their energy economies, such as the decarbonization underway in Germany. But Roberts said he can think of nothing comparable in the United States that has been successful at the scale and speed of change envisioned by most climate proposals. He is deeply skeptical of notions that coal miners will simply shift into clean-energy jobs at comparable pay.

"I don't see that happening. It certainly isn't happening now, and how it can happen in the future is beyond me."

Roberts is quick to point out that the UMWA has never doubted the reality of climate change or the need to address it. His complaint is that most of the proposed solutions seem to place the burden on the already disadvantaged to pay the price for change, while other, more well-to-do places reap most of the benefits. And while the United States appears to be turning away from coal, much of the developing world is not.

"So we've confined a lot of this pain, and a lot of this suffering, in order to deal in this country with climate change, to a geographic area that has suffered forever, economically," he said. "People are saying, what we need is a just transition. Well, we don't need a just transition for the future—we needed to have a just transition ten years ago, and no one came forward with a plan ten years ago to deal with what's happening in Appalachia."

THE SUBCOMMITTEE ON Energy and Mineral Resources met in February 2019 for its first hearing since the Democrats assumed control of the House. The hearing was titled "Climate Change: Preparing for the Energy Transition."[22] Witnesses included two men from community development groups in Appalachia: Peter Hille and Brandon Dennison.

Dennison was the founder of Coalfield Development, the West Virginia group where Danny Ferguson trains young workers and tries to create new opportunities. "We in Appalachia need to know we are valued," Dennison said in his statement to lawmakers, "and the country needs to know we have more to offer than just coal."

Just to Dennison's right sat Peter Hille, president of the Mountain Association for Community Economic Development, or MACED, based in Berea, Kentucky. Hille expanded on the idea of a just transition for his region. "The justice we call for in this transition is based on the reality that these communities and communities like ours literally fueled the growth of this great nation," he said. "They are owed a debt."

The lawmakers proceeded through the usual Kabuki theatrics of congressional hearings. Dennison and Hille made the trip back home to reflect on what, if anything, Congress might do with the advice they'd offered.

Hille has been with MACED for more than fifteen years. The organization started in 1976, not long after Hille first arrived in eastern Kentucky to run a church group project. "I fell in love with the place as only a young man can," he said, and he ended up staying.

MACED projects include sustainable agriculture, leadership training for community groups, and energy efficiency improvements. "This is an area full of smart, creative people doing remarkable things in spite of a deck that is stacked against them," he said.

Hille is a big proponent of the elegant solution, a single act that alleviates multiple problems. In a region with so many problems, you have to tackle more than one at a time just to keep up. Similarly, the discussion of a just transition and climate change must be about more than just replacing the few remaining coal jobs.

"Even if we could, we would just be where we were ten or fifteen years ago, and that's not going to do the trick," Hille said. "We were distressed then!"

It's a point that often gets glossed over in the rhetoric of a "coal comeback." Coal's decline has been underway for decades, and even during its heyday Appalachian communities had their share of problems.

Hille brings up the same economic concept that rural development expert Chuck Fluharty used to explain the region's situation: the "resource curse," sometimes called the "paradox of plenty." The paradox is that countries or regions blessed with resources often don't benefit from them. In fact, they often have reduced economic growth and little true development compared to other places. They frequently are less democratic and see higher levels of corruption and poverty.

There are many explanations for this. Extractive industries crowd out other investment, concentrate wealth for a few, and discourage growth of an entrepreneurial middle class. Education and infrastructure are undervalued and undeveloped. The excesses of extraction and the harms to human health and the natural world are ignored or justified as a necessary price for the region's sole sustenance. And then, of course, the whole system is vulnerable when the boom inevitably goes bust.

Every element of this is readily evident in Appalachian coal country, where each hill and holler offers up a fresh paradox of plenty. That is what Appalachia must overcome for a truly just transition, and it's certainly no small task. But such an approach would offer promise far beyond the rural towns Hille's group serves. America's great, intertwined challenges of reducing income inequality and achieving a clean-energy transition are on starkest display in these Appalachian communities, and solving them here could benefit us all.

"We need an economy that is not extractive but regenerative," Hille said. "We need to make these communities once again places where people want to live."

Acknowledgments

THE OHIO VALLEY ReSource team wishes to thank the newsrooms, staff, managers, and members at the partner stations that make up our journalism collaborative: Louisville Public Media; WEKU at Eastern Kentucky University; West Virginia Public Broadcasting; WKMS at Murray State University; WKU Public Radio at Western Kentucky University; WMMT at Appalshop; and WOUB at Ohio University.

The Ohio Valley ReSource was created with the support and vision of the Corporation for Public Broadcasting. Special thanks to Erin Day, Joy Lin, and Kathy Merritt at CPB for championing local public journalism.

We are grateful for our reporting partners at the Center for Public Integrity and NPR, especially NPR investigative reporter Howard Berkes, now retired, who consistently embodied the collaborative spirit in his approach to reporting.

Many scholars have helped us to better understand the history of the region and issues we cover, including Dr. Ron Eller, emeritus, University of Kentucky; Dr. Rosemary Feurer, Northern Illinois University; Dr. John Gaventa, University of Sussex; Dr. Gordon Lafer, University of Oregon; and Dr. Steven Stoll, Fordham University.

We thank the scientists, economists, researchers, writers, and reporters whose work has informed our journalism.

Thank you to Emily Carleton for your edits and patient guidance, and thanks to Sam Ford at Tiller Press for giving this book a shot.

Thank you to Rebecca Kiger, Roger May, and Jesse Wright for your photographs.

We thank our families and life partners for the extraordinary patience and understanding it takes to love and live with a journalist.

Finally, we thank the people of Appalachia and the Ohio Valley region, who gave us their time; shared with us their experiences, views, and ideas; and entrusted us to tell their stories.

The Ohio Valley ReSource team (left to right): Brittany Patterson, Jeff Young, Alexandra Kanik, Becca Schimmel, Liam Niemeyer, Sydney Boles, Aaron Payne, and Mary Meehan. Not pictured: Glynis Board and Benny Becker.

Contributors: The Reporters of the Ohio Valley ReSource

Jeff Young

Jeff is the ReSource managing editor and has reported from Appalachian coalfields, Capitol Hill, and New England's coast, among other places. Jeff worked for West Virginia Public Broadcasting and was Washington correspondent for the nationally distributed program *Living on Earth.* Jeff grew up near Huntington, West Virginia, and studied journalism and biology at Marshall University and the University of Charleston. He has received numerous awards for his reporting, and in 2012, he was named a Nieman Journalism Fellow at Harvard University.

Benny Becker

Benny reported on eastern Kentucky for the ReSource from 2016 to 2018 and remains an occasional contributor. Raised in Morgantown, West Virginia, Benny studied at Brown University and pursued radio and journalism in Rhode Island and Israel before returning to Appalachia. His reporting on black lung disease, in partnership with NPR's investigative team, won several awards, and in 2018 Benny was selected as one of the inaugural Abrams Nieman Fellows for Local Investigative Journalism at Harvard University.

Glynis Board

Glynis covered energy and environmental matters for the ReSource from 2016 to 2018 and remains an occasional contributor. She is acting news director at West Virginia Public Broadcasting, where she covers education and produces the daily news show *West Virginia Morning*. Glynis hails from the northern panhandle of West Virginia and is based in Wheeling. She's been reporting for West Virginia Public Broadcasting since 2012 and has won multiple regional and national journalism awards.

Sydney Boles

Sydney is the ReSource reporter covering the economic transition in the heart of Appalachia's coal country. Sydney received her master's degree in journalism from Medill School of Journalism, where she covered immigration and housing insecurity in Chicago. Sydney grew up in upstate New York, and before her work in journalism, she studied oral history and postcolonial resistance strategies in Costa Rica, India, South Africa, and Turkey.

Alexandra Kanik

Alexandra brings the numbers to life as the ReSource data reporter. Alexandra grew up in Pittsburgh and studied at the Maryland Institute College of Art. She began her career in journalism with PublicSource, a nonprofit news organization in Pittsburgh, as interactive developer and metrics analyst. The University of Michigan named Alexandra a finalist for the Livingston Awards for Young Journalists, which honors the best journalism professionals under the age of thirty-five.

Mary Meehan

Mary brings thirty years of experience to the health beat at the ReSource. Born in Kentucky, Mary is a proud alum of Western Kentucky University. A winner of dozens of state, regional, and national journalism awards, Mary has covered exploding hotels, trashed trailers, epic ER wait times, and one Santa convention. As a 2016 Nieman Fellow at Harvard University, Mary studied digital journalism and the challenge of using public health policy to create sustainable social change.

Liam Niemeyer

Liam covers agriculture and infrastructure for the ReSource, ranging from the burgeoning hemp industry to antiquated levee systems along the Ohio River. He grew up in central Ohio and first experienced life in Appalachia while studying at Ohio University in Athens, Ohio. He also serves as assistant news director for WKMS Public Radio in Murray, Kentucky. He brings experience in reporting across the country, having completed stints as a reporter and producer at Wyoming Public Radio, KRBD Community Radio in Alaska, WCPO-TV, WYSO Public Radio, and WOUB Public Media.

Aaron Payne

Aaron tackles the related issues of addiction recovery and economic recovery for the ReSource. He is a radio guy who first took to the airwaves at WMUL-FM, the campus voice for Marshall University, where he studied journalism. Aaron was the play-by-play voice of the West Virginia Miners baseball team (and he has the championship ring to prove it). At West Virginia Public Broadcasting he covered the state legislature and a chemical spill that left more than a quarter of a million people—including him—without potable water.

Brittany Patterson

Brittany is the ReSource reporter covering all things energy and environment. She most recently spent three years in Washington, DC, covering public lands and climate change for E&E News. A native of a hundred-person town in Northern California, she grew up working on her family's small organic farm and swimming in irrigation ditches. Brittany earned her bachelor's and master's degrees in journalism from San Jose State University and UC Berkeley, respectively.

Becca Schimmel

Becca's job is finding stories for the ReSource about the region's workforce, its rapidly changing economy, and the infrastructure of our built environment. She earned her journalism degree from Murray State University, where she has been a producer and general assignment reporter for WKMS. She has also worked on newspapers in Paducah and Marion, Kentucky. Becca grew up in Lexington, Kentucky.

Notes

Chapter 1. Welcome to Appalach-America

1. Appalachian Regional Commission, "County Economic Status in Appalachia, FY 2020," https://www.arc.gov/research/MapsofAppalachia.asp?MAP_ID=149.
2. L. Dwyer-Lindgren, A. Bertozzi-Villa, R. W. Stubbs, C. Morozoff, J. P. Mackenbach, C. J. L. Murray, F. J. van Lenthe, and A. H. Mokdad, "Inequalities in Life Expectancy Among US Counties, 1980 to 2014: Temporal Trends and Key Drivers," *JAMA Intern. Med.* 177, no. 7 (2017): 1003–11.
3. A. Morris, N. Kaufman, and S. Doshi, "The Risk of Fiscal Collapse in Coal-Reliant Communities," Center on Global Energy Policy, Columbia University/SIPA, July 15, 2019.
4. B. Becker, "Justice Delayed: Billionaire Candidate Owes $15M in Taxes and Fines," Ohio Valley ReSource, October 6, 2016.
5. B. Patterson, "Justice Dept. Seeks $4.7M in Mine Safety Debts from WV Gov. Justice's Family Coal Companies," Ohio Valley ReSource, May 7, 2019.
6. Z. Colman and L. Gardner, "Powerful Coal Executive Edges Closer to White House," *Politico*, March 30, 2019.
7. H. Berkes, H. Jingnan, and R. Benincasa, "An Epidemic Is Killing Thousands of Coal Miners. Regulators Could Have Stopped It,"

All Things Considered, December 18, 2018, https://www.npr.org/2018/12/18/675253856/an-epidemic-is-killing-thousands-of-coal-miners-regulators-could-have-stopped-it.

8. D. J. Blackley, C. N. Halldin, and A. S. Laney, "Continued Increase in Prevalence of Coal Workers' Pneumoconiosis in the United States, 1970–2017," *Am. J. Public Health* 108, no. 9 (2018): 1220–22.
9. T. Kuykendall and G. Dholakia, "US Coal Mining Employment Hits New Low at the End of 2019, May Go Lower in 2020," S&P Global Market Intelligence, Febuary 19, 2020.
10. US Energy Information Administration, "Short-Term Energy Outlook," December 10, 2019, https://www.eia.gov/outlooks/steo/report/coal.php.
11. M. Moulitsas, "Be Happy for Coal Miners Losing Their Health Insurance. They're Getting Exactly What They Voted For," *Daily Kos*, December 12, 2016.
12. K. Williamson, "The White Ghetto," *National Review*, December 16, 2013, https://www.nationalreview.com/2013/12/white-ghetto-kevin-d-williamson/.
13. M. Muro, R. Maxim, and J. Whiton, "Automation and Artificial Intelligence: How Machines Are Affecting People and Places," Brookings Institution, January 24, 2019, https://www.brookings.edu/research/automation-and-artificial-intelligence-how-machines-affect-people-and-places/.
14. A. Payne, "Investigation Finds Ohio Valley Hit Hard by Fentanyl as Locals Asked for More Federal Help," Ohio Valley ReSource, May 23, 2019.
15. A. Payne, "Ohio Valley Overdose Deaths Continue Grim Rise as Data Reflect Fentanyl's Role," Ohio Valley ReSource, July 27, 2018.
16. S. H. Woolf and H. Schoomaker, "Life Expectancy and Mortality Rates in the United States, 1959–2017," *JAMA* 322, no. 20 (2019): 1996–2016.
17. Federal Reserve Bank of Boston, "A House Divided: Geographic Disparities in Twenty-First Century America," 63rd Annual

Conference, October 4, 2019, https://www.bostonfed.org/housedivided2019/agenda.aspx.

18. P. Norris and R. Inglehart, *Cultural Backlash: Trump, Brexit, and Authoritarian Populism* (UK: Cambridge University Press, 2019).
19. S. Polakow-Suransky, *Go Back to Where You Came From: The Backlash Against Immigration and the Fate of Western Democracy* (New York: Bold Type Books, 2017).
20. J. A. Williams, *Appalachia: A History* (Chapel Hill: University of North Carolina Press, 2002).
21. R. Eller, *Uneven Ground: Appalachia Since 1945* (Lexington: University Press of Kentucky, 2013), 260.
22. B. Becker, M. Meehan, and J. Young, "Changing Course: A School Cooperative Aims to Remake Coal Communities," Ohio Valley ReSource, November 22, 2017.
23. A. Morris and N. Kaufman, "The Risk of Fiscal Collapse in Coal-Reliant Communities," Columbia SIPA Center on Global Energy Policy, Brookings Institution, July 2019, 31, https://www.brookings.edu/wp-content/uploads/2019/05/Morris_Kaufman_Doshi_RiskofFiscalCollapseinCoalReliantCommunities-CGEP_Report_FINAL.pdf.

Chapter 2. Bloody Harlan County: Then and Now

1. B. Patterson, "Judge Approves $5M Loan to Ailing Blackjewel Coal, but CEO Hoops Is Out," Ohio Valley ReSource, July 5, 2019.
2. B. Patterson and S. Boles, "Laid-Off Employees of Bankrupt Blackjewel Mining Seek Pay, Answers," Ohio Valley ReSource, July 10, 2019.
3. S. Boles and B. Patterson, "Blackjewel Miners Block Railroad to Demand Pay from Bankrupt Coal Company," Ohio Valley ReSource, July 30, 2019.
4. "Rosemary Feurer—NIU—Department of History," Northern Illinois University, n.d., https://www.niu.edu/history/about/faculty/feurer.shtml.

5. National Committee for the Defense of Political Prisoners, *Harlan Miners Speak: Report on Terrorism in the Kentucky Coal Fields*, with a new introduction by John C. Hennen (Lexington: University Press of Kentucky, 2008).
6. C. Collins and J. Hoxie, "Op-Ed: Jeff Bezos, Bill Gates and Warren Buffett Have More Wealth Than the Bottom Half of the Country Combined," *Los Angeles Times*, November 15, 2017.
7. J. Macey and J. Salovaara, "Bankruptcy as Bailout," *Stanford Law Review* 71, no 4 (April 2019): 879.
8. C. Lammers, "Hoops Family, City Announce Plans for Grand Patrician Resort in Milton," *Charleston Gazette-Mail*, October 12, 2017.
9. F. Pace, "Official: Grand Patrician Resort Project Not in Jeopardy," *Huntington Herald-Dispatch*, July 10, 2019.
10. B. Patterson and S. Boles, "Protesting Blackjewel Miners to Get Some Overdue Pay from Bankruptcy Sale," Ohio Valley ReSource, August 6, 2019.

Profile: Terry Steele

1. J. Young, "'Matewan' Revisited: Film Unearthed Region's Buried Labor History," Ohio Valley ReSource, October 6, 2017.
2. J. Young, "Still Fighting Labor's Historic Battle of Blair Mountain," *Living on Earth*, PRI, October 8, 2010, http://www.loe.org/shows/segments.html?programID=10-P13-00041&segmentID=3.
3. National Endowment for the Humanities, "WV Mine Wars Museum Gets $30,000 Grant," press release, September 4, 2019.
4. Hank Williams Jr., "I'm for Love," *Five-0*, Warner Bros. Records, May 1985.

Chapter 3. Coshocton's Power Switch

1. US Energy Information Administration, "US Coal Consumption in 2018 Expected to Be the Lowest in 39 Years," *Today in Energy*,

December 28, 2018, https://www.eia.gov/todayinenergy/detail.php?id=37817.

2. S. Feaster, "IEEFA Report: US Likely to End 2018 with Record Decline in Coal-Fired Capacity," *Institute for Energy Economics & Financial Analysis*, October 25, 2018, https://ieefa.org/ieefa-report-u-s-likely-to-end-2018-with-record-decline-in-coal-fired-capacity/.
3. G. J. Jolley, C. Khalaf, G. Michaud, and A. Sandler, "The Economic Fiscal and Workforce Impacts of Coal-Fired Power Plant Closures in Appalachian Ohio," *Regional Science Policy and Practice*, February 27, 2019, https://rsaiconnect.onlinelibrary.wiley.com/doi/abs/10.1111/rsp3.12191.
4. Muro, Maxim, and Whiton, "Automation and Artificial Intelligence."

Chapter 4. Pike County, Black Lung, and the Costs of Coal

1. H. Berkes, "Advanced Black Lung Cases Surge in Appalachia" *All Things Considered*, December 15, 2016, https://www.npr.org/2016/12/15/505577680/advanced-black-lung-cases-surge-in-appalachia.
2. D. J. Blackley, J. B. Crum, C. N. Halldin, E. Storey, and A. S. Laney, "Resurgence of Progressive Massive Fibrosis in Coal Miners: Eastern Kentucky, 2016," *Morbidity and Mortality Weekly Report* 65, no. 49 (2016): 1385–89, doi: http://dx.doi.org/10.15585/mmwr.mm6549a.
3. B. Becker, "Black Lung Update: Federal Researchers Seek Allies in Appalachia," Ohio Valley ReSource, April 4, 2017.
4. B. Becker, "Fighting for Breath: Black Lung's Deadliest Form Increases," Ohio Valley ReSource, December 16, 2016.
5. P. H. Rakes, "Black Lung Movement," *e-WV*, July 6, 2018.
6. J. Young, "Black Lung Is Back," *Living on Earth*, PRI, May 27, 2011, http://www.loe.org/shows/segments.html?programID=11-P13-00021&segmentID=1.

7. Berkes, Jingnan, and Benincasa, "An Epidemic Is Killing Thousands of Coal Miners."
8. US Department of Labor, Mine Safety and Health Administration, "Respirable Dust Rule: A Historic Step Forward in the Effort to End Black Lung Disease," August 1, 2014, https://www.msha.gov/news-media/special-initiatives/2016/09/28/respirable-dust-rule-historic-step-forward-effort-end.
9. B. Schimmel and J. Young, "Federal Prosecutor Charges Coal Company with Faking Dust Samples amid Black Lung Surge," Ohio Valley ReSource, July 11, 2018.
10. J. Young, "National Academy Report Urges Stronger Coal Dust Monitoring amid Black Lung Surge," Ohio Valley ReSource, June 28, 2018.
11. B. Becker, "Lung Transplants Rise amid Region's Black Lung Epidemic," Ohio Valley ReSource, May 16, 2018.
12. D. J. Blackley, C. N. Halldin, and A. S. Laney, "Continued Increase in Lung Transplantation for Coal Workers' Pneumoconiosis in the United States," *Am J. Ind Med.* 61 (2018): 621– 24, https://doi.org/10.1002/ajim.22856.
13. US Government Accountability Office, "Black Lung Benefits Program: Options for Improving Trust Fund Finances," May 30, 2018, https://www.gao.gov/products/GAO-18-351.
14. B. Schimmel and S. Boles, "Black Lung, Red Ink: Residents Press McConnell as Deadline Looms for Black Lung Fund," Ohio Valley ReSource, December 14, 2018.
15. H. Quinn, "Boost to Black-Lung Fund Unfair Burden on Mining Industry," *Lexington Herald-Leader*, December 4, 2018.
16. L. Friedman, "How a Coal Baron's Wish List Became President Trump's To-Do List," *New York Times*, January 9, 2018.
17. Hal Quinn to US Members of Congress, November 27, 2018, https://www.documentcloud.org/documents/5629082-National-Mining-Association-Hill-Letter-Nov-27.html.

18. S. Boles, "Still Fighting: These Widows' Stories Show Larger Effects of Black Lung Epidemic," Ohio Valley ReSource, January 18, 2019.
19. S. Boles, "As Calls for Action on Black Lung Disease Grow, Regulators Show Little Indication of Change," Ohio Valley ReSource, June 7, 2019.
20. B. Becker, "Amid Black Lung Surge, Kentucky Changes Benefits Process for Miners," Ohio Valley ReSource, March 28, 2018.
21. H. Berkes and B. Becker, "Kentucky Lawmakers Limit Black Lung Claims Reviews Despite Epidemic," *Weekend Edition*, NPR, March 31, 2018, https://www.npr.org/2018/03/31/598484688/kentucky-lawmakers-limit-black-lung-claims-reviews-despite-epidemic.
22. B. Becker, "Radiologists Call for Repeal of Kentucky Black Lung Law," Ohio Valley ReSource, April 6, 2018.
23. S. Boles, "Black Lung Benefits Drop for Kentucky Coal Miners after Controversial Law Change," Ohio Valley ReSource, February 21, 2020.
24. S. Boles, "New Kentucky Memorial Honors Miners Who Died of Black Lung," Ohio Valley ReSource, October 13, 2019.

Profile: Marcy Tate's New Beginnings

1. S. Boles, "Amid Black Lung Surge Pulmonary Rehab Brings Hope to Disabled Miners," Ohio Valley ReSource, December 18, 2018.

Chapter 5. Martin County Can't Get Clean Water

1. B. Becker, "Troubled Waters: A Coal County Loses Trust in Water and Government," Ohio Valley ReSource, January 27, 2017.
2. Ibid.
3. US Bureau of the Census, "QuickFacts: Martin County, Kentucky," https://www.census.gov/quickfacts/martincountykentucky.
4. M. Cromer and R. Draper, "Drinking Water Affordability Crisis: Martin County, Kentucky," report, Appalachian Citizens' Law

Center and Martin County Concerned Citizens, October 2019, https://appalachianlawcenter.org/wp-content/uploads/sites/10/2019/09/Drinking-Water-Affordability-Crisis-Martin-County-Kentucky-1.pdf.

5. American Society of Civil Engineers, "Making the Grade," Infrastructure Report Card, 2017, https://www.infrastructurereportcard.org/making-the-grade/.
6. B. Patterson, "Advocacy Group Finds Trace Contamination in Many Regional Water Systems," Ohio Valley ReSource, October 23, 2019.
7. Mine Safety and Health Administration and Office of Surface Mining, "Coal Waste Impoundments: Risks, Responses, and Alternatives," Report to Congress, August 15, 2013.
8. J. K. Bourne Jr., "Coal's Other Dark Side: Toxic Ash That Can Poison Water and People," *National Geographic*, February 19, 2019.
9. US Environmental Protection Agency, "Alpha Natural Resources Inc. Settlement," OECA, March 5, 2014, https://www.epa.gov/enforcement/alpha-natural-resources-inc-settlement.
10. B. Patterson and R. VanVelzer, "Coal Ash Uncovered: New Data Reveal Widespread Contamination at Ohio Valley Sites," Ohio Valley ReSource, June 18, 2018.
11. H. M. Caudill, *Night Comes to the Cumberlands: A Biography of a Depressed Area* (New York: Atlantic Monthly Press, 1963).
12. M. Hendryx, M. M. Ahern, and T. R. Nurkiewicz, "Hospitalization Patterns Associated with Appalachian Coal Mining," *J. Toxicol. Environ. Health A.* 70, no. 24 (2007): 2064–70.
13. M. Hendryx and M. M. Ahern, "Relations Between Health Indicators and Residential Proximity to Coal Mining in West Virginia," *Am. J. Pub. Health* 98, no. 4 (2008): 669–71.
14. S. Luanpitpong et al., "Appalachian Mountaintop Mining Particulate Matter Induces Neoplastic Transformation of Human

Bronchial Epithelial Cells and Promotes Tumor Formation," *Environmental Science and Technology* 48, no. 21 (October 2014): 12912–19.

15. M. Hendryx and M. M. Ahern, "Mortality in Appalachian Coal Mining Regions: The Value of Statistical Life Lost," *Public Health Reports* 124, no. 4 (July–August 2009): 541–50.
16. M. A. Palmer et al., "Mountaintop Mining Consequences," *Science,* January 8, 2010, 148–49.
17. B. Becker, "Mountains of Evidence: Questions about Coal's Most Controversial Practice May Finally Be Answered," Ohio Valley ReSource, September 2, 2016.
18. J. Tobias, "A Top DOI Official Had at Least Six Meetings with the Mining Industry. She Then Helped Cancel a Study on the Public-Health Effects of Mining," *Pacific Standard,* June 11, 2018.

Chapter 6. Tough Choices in Belmont County

1. B. Patterson, "Fracking's Next Boom? Petrochemical Plants Fuel Debate over Jobs, Pollution," Ohio Valley ReSource, November 30, 2018.
2. US Department of Energy, "Natural Gas Liquids Primer, with a Focus on the Appalachian Region," December 2017.
3. D. Bartz and V. Volcovici, "China Energy Executives Cancel West Virginia Trip amid Trade Dispute," Reuters, June 20, 2018.
4. B. Patterson, "As Ohio Valley Ponders Plastics Growth, Report Warns of Threat to Climate," Ohio Valley ReSource, May 15, 2019.
5. J. Zheng and S. Suh, "Strategies to Reduce the Global Carbon Footprint of Plastics," *Nature Climate Change,* April 15, 2019.
6. L. A. Hamilton et al., "Plastic and Climate: The Hidden Costs of a Plastic Planet," report, Center for International Environmental Law, May 2019.
7. J. J. Zou, "States Struggle to Deal with Radioactive Fracking Waste," Center for Public Integrity, June 17, 2016.

8. G. Board, "Hot Mess: How Radioactive Fracking Waste Wound Up Near Homes and Schools," Ohio Valley ReSource, June 17, 2016.
9. D. Dale, "Fact Check: Trump Takes Credit for Another Factory Approved Under Obama," CNN, August 15, 2019.
10. D. Dale and T. Subramaniam, "Donald Trump Made 84 False Claims Last Week," CNN, August 21, 2019.
11. US Energy Information Administration, "United States Remains the World's Top Producer of Petroleum and Natural Gas Hydrocarbons," *Today in Energy*, May 21, 2018, https://www.eia.gov/todayinenergy/detail.php?id=36292.
12. B. Patterson, "Settlement Reached over Proposed Ohio Cracker Plant Air Permit," Ohio Valley ReSource, September 23, 2019.
13. B. Patterson, "DOE Official Tells W.Va. Lawmakers Petrochemical Development Is a Top Priority," West Virginia Public Broadcasting, July 23, 2019.

Chapter 7. Clay City Faces Diseases of Despair

1. M. Meehan, "Leap of Faith: Religious Communities Reconsider Needle Exchanges," Ohio Valley ReSource, January 6, 2017.
2. A. Payne, "Born Addicted: The Race to Treat the Ohio Valley's Drug-Affected Babies," Ohio Valley ReSource, February 3, 2017.
3. P. Kocherlakota, "Neonatal Abstinence Syndrome," *Pediatrics* 134, no. 2 (2014): e547–61, doi:10.1542/peds.2013-3524.
4. A. Brill and S. Ganz, "The Geographic Variation in the Cost of the Opioid Crisis," American Enterprise Institute, March 2018.
5. Z. Zhang et al., "An Analysis of Mental Health and Substance Abuse Disparities and Access to Treatment Services in the Appalachian Region," report, Appalachian Regional Commission, August 2008, https://www.arc.gov/assets/research_reports/AnalysisofMentalHealthandSubstanceAbuseDisparities.pdf.

6. M. Meit, M. Heffernan, E. Tanenbaum, and T. Hoffmann, "Appalachian Diseases of Despair," report, NORC at the University of Chicago, August 2017, https://www.norc.org/Research/Projects/Pages/appalachian-diseases-of-despair.aspx.
7. E. Eyre, "Drug Firms Poured 780M Painkillers into WV amid Rise of Overdoses," *Charleston Gazette-Mail*, December 17, 2016.
8. M. M. Van Handel et al., "County-Level Vulnerability Assessment for Rapid Dissemination of HIV or HCV Infection Among Persons Who Inject Drugs, United States," *J. Acquired Immune Deficiency Syndromes* 73, no. 3 (2016): 323–31, doi:10.1097/QAI.0000000000001098.
9. M. Meehan, "Infection and Inequality: How the Income Gap Fuels Ohio Valley's Hep A Outbreak," Ohio Valley ReSource, July 27, 2018.
10. M. Meehan, "HIV Infection Clusters Put Focus on Harm Reduction Programs," Ohio Valley ReSource, August 16, 2019.
11. A. Payne, "Born Exposed: Schools Seek Ways to Help Children Exposed to Drugs in the Womb," Ohio Valley ReSource, September 20, 2019.
12. J. L. Oei et al., "Neonatal Abstinence Syndrome and High School Performance," *Pediatrics* 139, no. 2 (2017): e20162651.
13. M.-M. A. Fill et al., "Educational Disabilities Among Children Born with Neonatal Abstinence Syndrome," *Pediatrics* 142, no. 3 (2018): e20180562.
14. K. Willet, "UK, Kentucky Awarded $87 Million to Lead Effort in Combating Nation's Opioid Epidemic," University of Kentucky, April 18, 2019.

Profile: The Doctors Facing the Crisis

1. A. Payne, "The Doctor and the Epidemic: Three Years at Ground Zero of the Opioid Crisis," Ohio Valley ReSource, October 12, 2018.

2. A. Payne, "Painful Lessons: Using Data on Overdose Deaths to Combat Opioid Crisis," Ohio Valley ReSource, February 16, 2018.
3. A. Payne, "New Prescription: Ohio Valley Native Dr. Patrice Harris Is First Black Woman to Lead AMA," Ohio Valley ReSource, July 12, 2019.

Chapter 8. Growing a Recovery

1. L. Niemeyer, "Hemp's Heyday: It's Finally Legal. Now, Can Ohio Valley Farmers Cash In?" Ohio Valley ReSource, February 8, 2019.
2. L. Niemeyer, "CBD Uncertainty: Sales Soar But Science Lags on Hemp Health Effects," Ohio Valley ReSource, April 12, 2019.
3. L. Niemeyer, "Grassroots Growing: Hemp Farmers Form Cooperatives amid Growth and Uncertainty," Ohio Valley ReSource, October 11, 2019.
4. J. Young, "J. D. Vance Investor Tour Draws Hopeful Companies and Harsh Critics," Ohio Valley ReSource, May 9, 2018.
5. J. Fox, "Venture Capital Keeps Flowing to the Same Places," *Bloomberg*, January 8, 2019.
6. S. Jones and J. D. Vance, "The False Prophet of Blue America," *New Republic*, November 17, 2016.
7. L. Niemeyer and B. Patterson, "A Growing Recovery: Food Service and Farming Jobs Provide a Path Out of Addiction," Ohio Valley ReSource, May 17, 2019.

Chapter 9. Politicoal 1: Justice Delayed

1. B. McElhinny, "Justice on Trump: 'His Attraction to West Virginia Is Me. That's It,'" *MetroNews*, June 14, 2019.
2. L. Debter, "Meet the Richest Person in Every State, 2018," *Forbes*, May 21, 2018.
3. J. Taylor and S. Detrow, "West Virginia Governor Announces He'll Switch to GOP at Trump Rally," NPR, August 3, 2017.

4. B. Estep, "Companies Run by Billionaire Candidate for W. Va. Governor Owe Millions in Delinquent Taxes in Ky," *Lexington Herald-Leader*, October 12, 2015.
5. B. Becker, "Justice Delayed: Billionaire Candidate's Coal Companies Owe $15M in Taxes, Fines," Ohio Valley ReSource, October 6, 2016.
6. H. Berkes, "Billionaire Gubernatorial Candidate Owes $15 Million in Taxes and Fines," NPR, October 7, 2016.
7. Patterson, "Justice Dept. Seeks $4.7M in Overdue Mine Safety Fines from WV Gov. Justice's Family Companies."
8. Becker, "Justice Delayed."
9. D. Mistich, "WV Gov. Justice Says His Company's Delinquent Taxes Are Now Paid in His State," West Virginia Public Broadcasting, August 6, 2018.
10. J. Young, "Rural Counties Under Stress from Justice Companies' Unpaid Taxes in Several States," Ohio Valley ReSource, August 8, 2018.
11. Ibid.
12. B. Patterson, "Coal Companies Belonging to WV Gov. Justice's Family Agree to Pay Overdue Taxes in KY," Ohio Valley ReSource, June 11, 2019.
13. H. Berkes, A. Boiko-Weyrauch, and R. Benincasa, "Special Series. Delinquent Mines: Billionaire Spent Millions in Charity, but Avoided Mine Fines," NPR, November 15, 2014.
14. Becker, "Justice Delayed."
15. A. Kanik and B. Patterson, "Mine Safety Debt for WV Gov. Justice's Family Companies Grows to $4M," Ohio Valley ReSource, April 5, 2019.
16. US Attorney's Office, Western District of Virginia, "United States Files Civil Action to Collect Debts Owed for Violations of Federal Mine Safety Act," press release, May 7, 2019, https://www.justice.gov/usao-wdva/pr/united-states-files-civil-action-collect-debts-owed-violations-federal-mine-safety-act.

17. Patterson, "Justice Dept. Seeks $4.7M in Overdue Mine Safety Fines from WV Gov. Justice's Family Companies."
18. B. Patterson, "Justice Coal Companies Agree to Settle $5 Million in Delinquent Mine Safety Debts," Ohio Valley ReSource, April 1, 2020.
19. B. Patterson, "Idle Lands: Justice Coal Group Top User of Loophole Allowing Mine Lands to Sit Idle," Ohio Valley ReSource, September 4, 2019.
20. M. Olalde and J. Yerardi, "While 'Zombie' Mines Idle, Cleanup and Workers Remain in Limbo," Center for Public Integrity, September 4, 2019.
21. B. Estep and W. Wright, "Kentucky Coal Helped W.Va. Governor Prosper. Now a Bitter Fight over the Aftermath," *Lexington Herald-Leader*, August 19, 2018.
22. Becker, "Justice Delayed."
23. S. Boles, "KY Coal Mine That Belonged to WV Governor Causes Damaging Floods Again," Ohio Valley ReSource, November 2, 2018.
24. Ibid.

Chapter 10. Politicoal 2: Trump Country Revisited

1. "Bill Raney, President WVCA, Receives Communicator Award from Careers in Coal," CoalZoom.com, April 29, 2019.
2. J. Young, "Passing the Test," *Living on Earth*, PRI, January 16, 2009, http://www.loe.org/shows/segments.html?programID=09-P13-00003&segmentID=2.
3. T. Houser, J. Bordoff, and P. Marsters, "Can Coal Make a Comeback?" Center on Global Energy Policy, April 2017.
4. G. Board, "A Coal Comeback? Analysis Casts Doubt on Industry's Chances," Ohio Valley ReSource, May 10, 2017.
5. B. Patterson, "Coal Comeback? Coal at New Low After Two Years Under Trump," Ohio Valley ReSource, February 1, 2019.
6. US Energy Information Administration, "Short-Term Energy Outlook," December 10, 2019, https://www.eia.gov/outlooks/steo/report/coal.php.

7. B. Patterson, "Ohio-Based Coal Giant Murray Energy Declares Bankruptcy," Ohio Valley ReSource, October 29, 2019.
8. J. Young, "Miner Safety Getting Shafted?" *Living on Earth*, PRI, October 5, 2007, http://www.loe.org/shows/segments.html?programID=07-P13-00040&segmentID=2.
9. B. Patterson, "Murray Energy Loses Appeal over Miner Intimidation Case," West Virginia Public Broadcasting, May 7, 2019.
10. J. Mouawad, "A Crusader in the Coal Mine, Taking on President Obama," *New York Times*, April 30, 2016.
11. S. Boles, "Murray Energy CEO Lashes Out at 'Feckless' Federal Officials over Coal Subsidy Plan," Ohio Valley ReSource, October 22, 2019.
12. J. Young and A. Kanik, "Trumped: Coal's Collapse, Economic Anxiety Motivated Ohio Valley Voters," Ohio Valley ReSource, November 18, 2016.
13. C. Ingraham, "Where People Show Up to Vote—and Where They Don't," *Washington Post*, October 15, 2018.
14. E. Catte, "Appalachia Isn't the Reason We're Living in Trump Country," *Literary Hub*, February 8, 2018.
15. G. Pillsbury and J. Johannesen, eds., "America Goes to the Polls 2016: A Report on Voter Turnout in the 2016 Election," Nonprofit Vote and the US Elections Project, March 2017, https://www.nonprofitvote.org/documents/2017/03/america-goes-polls-2016.pdf/.
16. A. Liptak, "Supreme Court Upholds Ohio's Purge of Voting Rolls," *New York Times*, June 11, 2018.
17. "Voting Rights Restoration Efforts in Kentucky," Brennan Center for Justice, November 7, 2018, https://www.brennancenter.org/our-work/research-reports/voting-rights-restoration-efforts-kentucky.
18. J. Bartle, S. Birch, and M. Skirmuntt, "The Local Roots of the Participation Gap: Inequality and Voter Turnout," *Electoral Studies* 48 (August 2017): 30–44.

19. J. Galbraith and J. Hale, "State Income Inequality and Presidential Election Turnout and Outcomes," *Social Science Quarterly* 98 (February 2008): 887–901, doi:10.1111/j.1540-6237.2008.00589.x.
20. J. L. Brown-Iannuzzi, K. B. Lundberg, and S. McKee, "Political Action in the Age of High-Economic Inequality: A Multilevel Approach," *Social Issues and Policy Review* 11, no. 1 (2016): 232–73.

Profile: Carl and Scott Shoupe

1. L. M. Sutter, *Ball, Bat and Bitumen: A History of Coalfield Baseball in the Appalachian South* (Jefferson, NC: McFarland Publishers, 2008), 138.

Chapter 11. Coal, Climate, and Just What "Just Transition" Means

1. US Bureau of the Census, "QuickFacts: Lincoln County, West Virginia," https://www.census.gov/quickfacts/fact/table/lincolncountywestvirginia/PST045218.
2. G. Board, "Picturing the Future: A Coal Community's Comeback," Ohio Valley ReSource, December 23, 2016.
3. B. Becker, "Coal Country Tech Job Program Heads for New Round," Ohio Valley ReSource, August 29, 2017.
4. B. Becker and J. Young, "Defunding Appalachia: Coal Communities Resist President's Budget Cuts," Ohio Valley ReSource, March 24, 2017.
5. B. Schimmel, "McConnell Aide Takes Appalachian Regional Commission Role," Ohio Valley ReSource, April 24, 2018.
6. US Office of the Press Secretary, "Fact Sheet: The Partnerships for Opportunity and Workforce and Economic Revitalization (POWER) Initiative," March 27, 2015, https://obamawhitehouse.archives.gov/the-press-office/2015/03/27/fact-sheet

-partnerships-opportunity-and-workforce-and-economic
-revitaliz.

7. "Appalachian Regional Commission Announces $44.4 Million to Diversify Region's Coal-Impacted Economies," press release, Appalachian Regional Commission, October 2019.
8. Eller, *Uneven Ground*, 180–81.
9. Ibid., 190.
10. G. Board, "The New Normal: Super Storms Highlight Importance of Disaster Planning," Ohio Valley ReSource, September 22, 2017.
11. R. Leven and Z. Goldstein, "A Disastrous Disconnect," Center for Public Integrity, October 28, 2019.
12. K. Hayhoe et al., "Our Changing Climate," in *Climate Change Impacts in the United States: The Third National Climate Assessment*, ed. J. M. Melillo, T. Richmond, and G. W. Yohe (Washington, DC: USGCRP/GCIS, 2014), 19–67, doi:10.7930/J0KW5CXT.
13. T. R. Karl, J. T. Melillo, T. C. Peterson, and S. J. Hassol, eds., *Global Climate Change Impacts in the United States* (UK: Cambridge University Press, 2009).
14. G. Board, "The Flood Next Time: Warming Raises the Risk of Disaster," Ohio Valley ReSource, July 22, 2016.
15. B. Patterson, "Trump Administration Replaces Obama-Era Climate Change Rule on Power Plants," Ohio Valley ReSource, June 19, 2019.
16. M. Mildenberger et al., "The Spatial Distribution of Republican and Democratic Climate Opinions at State and Local Scales," *Climatic Change* 145, no. 4 (December 2017): 539, doi:10.1007/s10584-017-2103-0.
17. J. Marlon et al., "Yale Climate Opinion Maps 2019," Yale Program on Climate Change Communication, September 17, 2019.
18. A. Morris, N. Kaufman, and S. Doshi, "The Risk of Fiscal Collapse in Coal-Reliant Communities," report, Brookings Institution, July

15, 2019, https://www.brookings.edu/research/the-risk-of-fiscal-collapse-in-coal-reliant-communities/.

19. "A Green New Deal Must Be Rooted in a Just Transition for Workers and Communities Most Impacted by Climate Change," press release, Climate Justice Alliance, December 10, 2018.
20. S. Horsley, "Fact Check: Hillary Clinton and Coal Jobs," NPR, May 3, 2016.
21. E. Relman, "Hillary Clinton: Here's the Misstep from the Campaign I Regret Most," *Business Insider*, September 6, 2017.
22. B. Patterson, "Coal Community Leaders Urge Congress to Include Them in Climate Action," Ohio Valley ReSource, February 12, 2019.

Photo Credits

p. 7: Courtesy of the Appalachian Regional Commission; map by Alexandra Kanik.

p. 9: Photo courtesy of Becca Schimmel.

p. 11: Courtesy of the Appalachian Regional Commission; graphic by Alexandra Kanik.

p. 22: Photo courtesy of Sydney Boles.

p. 30: Photo courtesy of Becca Schimmel.

p. 42: Courtesy of the US Energy Information Administration; graphic by Alexandra Kanik.

p. 45: Courtesy of the US Energy Information Administration; graphic by Alexandra Kanik.

p. 53: Photo courtesy of J. Tyler Franklin, Louisville Public Media.

p. 61: Photo courtesy of Benny Becker.

p. 65: Photo courtesy of Adelina Lancianese, NPR.

p. 79: Photo courtesy of Sydney Boles.

p. 81: Photo courtesy of Marcy Tate.

p. 85: Photo courtesy of Benny Becker.

p. 100: Photo courtesy of Sydney Boles.

p. 107: Photo courtesy of Brittany Patterson.

p. 121: Courtesy of the NORC at the University of Chicago.

p. 126: Photo courtesy of Mary Meehan.

p. 130: Courtesy of the Kentucky Cabinet for Health and Family Services, Ohio Department of Health, West Virginia Department of Health and Human Resources; graphic by Alexandra Kanik.

p. 141: Photo courtesy of Liam Lienmeyer.

p. 148: Photo courtesy of Brittany Patterson.

p. 153: Photo courtesy of Jesse Wright, West Virginia Public Broadcasting.

p. 160: Photo courtesy of Brittany Patterson.

p. 166: Photo courtesy of Sydney Boles.

p. 171: Courtesy of the Mine Safety and Health Administration; graphic by Alexandra Kanik.

p. 183: Photo courtesy of Scott Shoupe.

p. 189: Photo courtesy of Rebecca Kiger.

p. 192: Courtesy of the US Census Bureau American Community Survey Five-year 2017; graphic by Alexandra Kanik.

p. 206: Photo courtesy of J. Tyler Franklin, Louisville Public Media.

Index